DRAMA CLASS

T0276706

The Drama Classics series aims to offer the great plays in affordable paperback editions for students, actors and theatregoers. The hallmarks of the series are accessible introductions, uncluttered texts and an overall theatrical perspective.

Given that readers may be encountering a particular play for the first time, the introduction seeks to fill in the theatrical/historical background and to outline the chief themes rather than concentrate on interpretational and textual analysis. Similarly the play-texts themselves are free of footnotes and other interpolations: instead there is an end-glossary of 'difficult' words and phrases.

The texts of the English-language plays in the series have been prepared taking full account of all existing scholarship. The foreign-language plays have been newly translated into a modern English that is both actable and accurate: many of the translators regularly have their work staged professionally.

Edited until his early death by Kenneth McLeish, the Drama Classics series continues with his aim of providing a first-class library of dramatic literature representing the best of world theatre.

Associate editors:
Professor Trevor R. Griffiths
Honorary Professor in Humanities, University of Exeter
Dr Colin Counsell
Senior Lecturer in Theatre Studies and Performing Arts

DRAMA CLASSICS *the first hundred*

The Alchemist
All for Love
Andromache
Antigone
Bacchae
Bartholomew Fair
The Beaux Stratagem
The Beggar's Opera
Birds
Blood Wedding
Celestina
The Changeling
A Chaste Maid in
 Cheapside
The Cherry Orchard
Children of the Sun
El Cid
The Country Wife
The Dance of Death
The Devil is an Ass
Doctor Faustus
A Doll's House
Don Juan
The Duchess of
 Malfi
Edward II
Electra (Euripides)
Electra (Sophocles)
An Enemy of the
 People
Everyman
Faust
A Flea in her Ear
Frogs
Fuente Ovejuna
The Game of Love
 and Chance
Ghosts
The Government
 Inspector
Hecuba
Hedda Gabler

The Hypochondriac
The Importance of
 Being Earnest
An Ideal Husband
An Italian Straw Hat
Ivanov
The Jew of Malta
The Knight of the
 Burning Pestle
The Lady from the Sea
The Learned Ladies
Lady Windermere's
 Fan
Life is a Dream
London Assurance
The Lower Depths
The Lucky Chance
Lulu
Lysistrata
The Malcontent
The Man of Mode
The Marriage of
 Figaro
Mary Stuart
The Master Builder
Medea
The Misanthrope
The Miser
Miss Julie
A Month in the
 Country
Oedipus
The Oresteia
Peer Gynt
Phedra
The Playboy of the
 Western World
The Recruiting
 Officer
The Revenger's
 Tragedy
The Rivals

The Roaring Girl
La Ronde
Rosmersholm
The Rover
Scapino
The School for
 Scandal
The Seagull
The Servant of Two
 Masters
She Stoops to Conquer
The Shoemakers'
 Holiday
Six Characters in Search
 of an Author
The Spanish Tragedy
Spring Awakening
Summerfolk
Tartuffe
Three Sisters
'Tis Pity She's a
 Whore
Too Clever by Half
Ubu
Uncle Vanya
Volpone
The Way of the
 World
The White Devil
The Wild Duck
A Woman of No
 Importance
Women Beware
 Women
Women of Troy
Woyzeck
Yerma

*The publishers welcome
suggestions for further titles*

DRAMA CLASSICS

LIFE
IS A DREAM

by

Pedro Calderón de la Barca

translated and with an introduction by
John Clifford

NICK HERN BOOKS

London
www.nickhernbooks.co.uk

A Drama Classic

Life is a Dream first published in Great Britain in this translation as a paperback original in 1998 by Nick Hern Books Limited, 14 Larden Road, London W3 7ST

Reprinted 2000, 2001, 2003, 2005, 2007, 2011

Copyright in this translation © 1998 John Clifford
Copyright in the introduction © 1998 Nick Hern Books

Typeset by Country Setting, Woodchurch, Kent TN26 3TB
Printed by CLE Print Ltd, St Ives, Cambs, PE27 3LE

A CIP catalogue record for this book is available from the British Library

ISBN 978 1 85459 188 3

Introduction

Pedro Calderón de la Barca (1600-81)

Calderón was born in Madrid on 17 January 1600. His father was a senior official in the government. The family had pretensions to nobility; but in Spain's racially obsessed society the profession of administrator, secretary or official was a somewhat dubious one. Those who exercised such professions were tainted with the suspicion that they might be of Jewish or Muslim origin; so Calderón's family's social standing can never have been a secure one.

Pedro Calderón was the third of six brothers; their love and support for each other seems to have been vital in a troubled life. Their mother died in childbirth when Calderón was ten; in 1614, four years later, his father married again. The stepmother hated the brothers so intensely that when their father died in 1615 she initiated a successful lawsuit that left them disinherited and dispossessed.

The father, to judge both from the terms of his will and the portrayal of fathers in his son's plays, was authoritarian and unloving. He stipulated that on pain of disinheritance his eldest son must abandon his relationship with the woman he loved and wished to marry. As for Pedro, he ordered him on no account to abandon his studies and commanded him to become a priest.

Calderón's response to this was to leave university, abandon the calling to priesthood and embrace the dissolute and disreputable profession of poet and playwright. Once his first successful play, *Love, Honour and Power*, was performed in 1625, he rapidly built up for himself a reputation as a poet, a dramatist and a wit.

He and his brothers were also building up a dubious reputation as brawlers and duellists, implicated in the deaths of several men and the violation of a convent. They narrowly escaped prison on more than one occasion; and for a couple of years Calderón had to live in exile.

It was probably in the late 1620s, in the midst of this troubled and turbulent period, that he wrote *Life is a Dream*. Scattered references to it in other plays indicate that the play took a hold of the imagination both of fellow playwrights and of audiences; when he and his brother came to publish the first volume of his Plays (in 1636) he placed it at the head of the volume.

At that time, theatre in Spain was still dominated by the extraordinary skills of Lope de Vega and, to a lesser degree, his rival Tirso de Molina. Tirso, who was a member of a religious order, was silenced in 1625 (he was exiled to a remote monastery and deprived of pen and paper) and Lope's death in 1635 left the way clear for Calderón to establish himself as the leading playwright of his day.

From then until his death in 1681, he kept on writing an astonishing stream of beautiful plays in all three dramatic arenas open to him – in the public theatre, the court theatre, and in the street, where his *auto sacramentales* were performed during the feast of Corpus Christi. These allegorical dramas were played on carts equipped with extraordinary and ingenious stage machinery, and they generally dramatised points of Catholic doctrine.

Though the *auto sacramental* sounds like a distinctly unpromising type of drama, Calderón wrote for it plays of miraculous intellect, wit, dramatic imagination and human tenderness.

He also mastered the art of writing spectacle for the royal court. Philip IV loved theatre, and built several in his palaces. He commissioned elaborately staged spectacles from Calderón, often based on mythological subjects.

Philip IV was king only in name; the real power was wielded by his chief minister, Olivares, who encouraged Philip's love of pleasure and theatrical spectacle, because the appeal of these distractions made it easier for Olivares to exercise control over the important affairs of state.

Knowingly or not, Calderón participated in this process. The fall of Olivares in 1643 left him in some difficulty; and his direct experiences of war, fighting in the army involved in the suppression of the revolt of Catalonia in 1640, all deepened his disillusionment with Spain's militaristic policies as it attempted to hold on to its rapidly dissolving empire.

But neither these setbacks, nor the deaths of his brothers, nor an affair with an unnamed woman prevented Calderón from writing plays. In 1647 his only son was born; in 1651 he became a priest; in 1657 the son died. And Calderón kept on writing plays. He was writing till the day of his death, on 25 May 1681, and in his will he wrote the script for his own funeral. He was very specific about the costumes of his pallbearers and his own corpse, and insisted the coffin be kept open so that his corpse could be seen as it was dragged through the streets of Madrid. He hoped the public would learn from the spectacle – and think about how best to lead their lives.

His Plays

His work remains largely unknown to this day.

In the past twenty years in Britain very little of it has been seen: *Life is a Dream* (by the RSC in a very free adaptation by Adrian Mitchell), *The Mayor of Zalamea* (by the National Theatre), *Schism in England* (my translation; again by the National), *The Doctor of Honour* (by Cheek by Jowl), a brave and wonderful attempt at one of his *autos*, *The Great Theatre of the World* by the Medieval Players and recently *The Painter of His Dishonour* by the RSC in a fine translation by David Johnstone.

So much still remains to be discovered:

Devotion to the Cross, a passionate flirtation with incest and parricide;

The Constant Prince, a deeply moving meditation on the virtue (or stupidity) of martyrdom;

The Statue of Prometheus, an extraordinary retelling of the myth;

The Amazing Magician, his version of the Faust legend;

. . . and even this list (which is very selective) leaves out his comedies.

I translated his brilliantly funny *House with Two Doors* in 1980 (the experience helped me discover myself as a playwright) and continue to be astonished that plays like *The Veiled Lady and the Hidden Man*, *The Female Ghost*, *True Love Burns like Fire*, *Nothing Is More Powerful Than Silence* remain completely unknown. They rival Goldoni in their ingenuity, and surpass him in wit, theatrical flair and sheer humanity.

There can be few writers who gave so much to their chosen form: and yet who still remain so unknown for it.

What Happens In the Play

Act One

Rosaura enters dressed as a man. Her horse has bolted and left her and her servant Clarín utterly lost in a mountainous region when night is falling. They see a tower and go up to it, hoping to find shelter. Instead they find a naked chained man imprisoned in a dark tower. He does not understand why he has been imprisoned: he and Rosaura feel a profound attraction for each other.

The prisoner's jailer, Clotaldo, arrests Rosaura and Clarín for trespassing on forbidden ground. Rosaura hands him her sword; and he recognises it. It was once his: he gave it to his lover and made her promise that she should give it to their child.

Clotaldo is now caught in a dilemma: he has been ordered to kill all those who approach the tower, and he cannot bear the thought of killing his own child.

We move to the court of Poland, where Astolfo and Estrella are beginning to woo each other. We learn that Basilio, the king, is childless; Astolfo and Estrella are his nephew and niece, and he is encouraging them to marry in order to settle their competing claims for the throne.

Estrella remarks that Astolfo's declarations of love are not particularly convincing; not least since he is wearing the portrait of another woman hanging around his neck. Astolfo's explanations are cut short by the arrival of the king.

Basilio complacently reminds his nephew, his niece and his whole court of his skill as an astrologer and his capacity to foretell future events. He then recalls his dismay at the appalling horoscope that he read at his son's birth. It foretold civil war between father and son and his own eventual defeat. His wife died in childbirth; unwilling to kill his own child, Basilio nonetheless felt unable to ignore his horoscope. At the time, it was announced the son had been born dead; Basilio tells his court that in fact Segismundo is alive.

He is the prisoner in the tower, and has been kept in isolation since the day he was born. Tomorrow, Basilio intends to make a test of Segismundo's capacity for kingship: he will be brought from the tower to take Basilio's place in the palace. Everything he orders will be carried out as if he were king. If Segismundo responds to this situation with wisdom and self-restraint, then he will be crowned king. If not, he will be deposed, sent back to the tower, and the succession will pass to Astolfo and Estrella.

Leaving his courtiers to digest this sensational piece of news, Basilio is met by Clotaldo. Clotaldo is about to beg for his child's life when Basilio instructs him to free the prisoners. There is no more need to keep Segismundo's existence a secret.

Rosaura and Clotaldo, meanwhile, are intensely curious about each other's identity. Rosaura is looking for her father; Clotaldo wants to know more about his child. He manages to draw out of Rosaura the fact that she is his daughter; that she has been seduced and abandoned by Astolfo, and has followed him to Poland to seek revenge.

Act Two

The act begins with Clotaldo telling Basilio that Segismundo has been drugged and brought to the palace. Basilio explains that if Segismundo fails this test of character, he can be drugged again and taken back to his prison, and then told that everything he saw in the palace was nothing but a dream.

Clotaldo has huge misgivings about the whole project; but it's all too late, because Segismundo has already woken up. Basilio instructs Clotaldo to tell him he is the son of the king.

Segismundo, who has spent all his life a prisoner, bound in chains, is utterly bewildered by the change in his fortunes. He becomes very angry when he discovers he's actually the son of a king, and tries to kill Clotaldo, the man who's been keeping him in prison. When a servant tries to reason with him, Segismundo kills him; when he sees Rosaura – who is now wearing women's clothes – he tries to rape her; when Clotaldo intervenes Segismundo tries to kill first Clotaldo and then Astolfo. He is furious with his own father, whom he insults; and it is obvious he is going to have to be drugged again and returned to prison.

Clarín meets Clotaldo and blackmails him into giving him money and a position in return for agreeing not to disclose Rosaura's identity.

Rosaura, who has been advised by Clotaldo to dress as a woman to avoid scandal, has become a lady-in-waiting to Estrella until her situation improves. Estrella sends her to Astolfo to pick up the portrait he has been wearing and that so offended her the last time they met. It is obviously Rosaura's portrait; and she is placed in an impossible position. Astolfo recognises her at once; Rosaura manages to trick him out of her portrait and place him in the wrong before Estrella.

Segismundo is returned to the tower; Clarín is imprisoned alongside him to thwart his blackmail. Just before leaving him alone with his chains, Clotaldo advises Segismundo to try to control his rage; life may be a dream, but the good you do is never lost. Not even in dreams.

Segismundo is left alone. He tries to understand what has happened to him; and concludes that the whole of life is nothing but a dream.

Act Three

Clarín is still in the tower. He's hungry, and he keeps having bad dreams. He is astonished when a group of soldiers burst in, call him Prince Segismundo, and ask him to rule them. It's obviously what they do in Poland – some kind of weird custom – and he's about to do as they say when Segismundo appears. The soldiers explain they are in rebellion against Basilio. They've learnt he has a son whom they want to be their king. They don't want Astolfo.

Segismundo is reluctant to go with them. He's convinced it's all going to turn out to be just another dream, and he'll end up back in the tower feeling even worse than before. But the soldiers persuade him; and he promises himself he'll try to remember that it is only a dream and not get carried away with it. They all set off to march against the palace of the king.

When the rebellion breaks out, Clotaldo expects Segismundo to kill him; but Segismundo has taken his words to heart, and is trying to do good. So he lets Clotaldo go free. When he reaches the palace, Clotaldo discovers the rebellion has spread throughout the kingdom. Basilio is in despair: he understands that he has brought about the very thing he set out to try to prevent.

There is nothing to be done but try to crush the rebellion: he, Astolfo, and Estrella set out to fight. Rosaura prevents Clotaldo following them; she still wants revenge on Astolfo, and she wants to discover if Clotaldo is her father. Clotaldo tries to evade the whole issue by suggesting Rosaura enter a convent; Rosaura refuses. She sets off to fight for Segismundo. Clotaldo goes off to fight for the king.

Segismundo, meanwhile, is marching with his army, exhilarated by their success. Rosaura reaches him, and tells him her story. The first time she met him dressed as a man; the second, dressed as a woman; now she meets him dressed as an androgyne, wearing both a gorgeous dress and the weapons of war. She has come both to help him fight his battle and obtain his help in her quest for revenge.

Seeing her again, Segismundo is able to connect all the different parts of his experience. He finally understands that what he saw in the palace was not a dream; that life has reality and substance. He really desires Rosaura and is tempted to rape her. But he remembers Clotaldo's words about doing good. They seem to be the only thread that can help him make sense of life's confusion.

The only way he can overcome his desire for Rosaura is turn his back on her; he marches off to war, leaving her uncertain and confused. Clarín rejoins her and is just about to tell her that Clotaldo is her father when the battle begins. Rosaura goes off to fight; Clarín isn't going to be so silly as to fight. He'll escape death by hiding.

Basilio is defeated; in his flight he stumbles across the dying Clarín, who has been hit by a stray shot. It seems to Clarín that his attempt to hide from death has just brought him straight into the path of the bullet; and his dying words remind Basilio of his responsibility for his own misfortune. He, too, has been running from death: he resolves to wait for Segismundo and meet death face to face.

But Segismundo does not kill his father. Instead he begs his forgiveness, and they become reconciled. Basilio reaffirms his choice of Segismundo as the new king.

Segismundo marries Rosaura to Astolfo, and marries Estrella himself. He rewards Clotaldo, and when the soldier who started the rebellion asks what reward he's going to get, Segismundo imprisons him for life. Everyone is amazed at the change in him: but Segismundo admits he is still terrified it is still all going to turn out to be a dream.

The Theatre

There were two public theatres in Madrid at the time *Life is a Dream* was first performed. Both put on a play a day during the season. Because they were outdoors, performances began in the early afternoon and ended before nightfall.

The theatres were rectangular yards with a thrust stage at one end, with windows and balconies built into the adjoining houses to allow for a view of the stage. Ticket prices varied to allow entrance to all classes of society. The cheapest gave access to the standing area in front of the stage; those prepared to pay more could sit on tiered benches beside it. There were spaces for the nobility, for representatives of the city council; a special box directly opposite the stage was reserved for women. They had their own special entrance to the theatre, with a guard to prevent them being harassed as they went in. Above them was a box reserved for priests and monks; and it was rumoured that often performances were attended incognito by king Philip IV himself.

So plays attracted every social class; and the play itself was only a part of the diverse entertainment on offer in an afternoon at the theatre. The performance began with a piece of instrumental music, or a song; then came the prologue, or *loa*, which sometimes consisted of one actor speaking a prologue, usually containing in-jokes aimed at each particular audience, and sometimes of a more elaborate playlet or sketch.

There is one that survives that relates very directly to this play: the director (and main actor) of the company is shown fast asleep under a tree, dreaming of full money bags. But like most theatre directors before or since when he wakes up he discovers the moneybags are empty. His wealth was just a dream; 'and dreams are only dreams'.

So when the first act of the play proper began, the audience were already warmed up and receptive. At the end of the first act, they watched a short farce or *entremés;* a dance at the end of the second; and at the end of the third another farce and possibly more music and dance.

The stage on which all this was performed was simple and flexible. It had two entrances, one on each side, each covered with curtains. In the centre, again covered with a curtain, was a recess or discovery space where Segismundo, for instance, is discovered in his prison.

Above this was a balcony, which could serve as the upper storey of a house, or (as in this play) the top of a mountain. Painted panels could be fixed to it, to represent trees, mountain crags or whatever was necessary; and in this play a set of steps would be fixed in place to allow Rosaura to climb down her mountain at the beginning of the play.

The very top storey could be used to mount stage machinery for flying clouds, angels, etc., on special occasions.

Changes of scene were indicated by simple changes of costume (such as wearing a cloak to signify outdoors) or the use of emblematic props. A light brought onto the (brilliantly sunlit) stage, for instance, signified night-time. If someone blew out the light, then everybody immediately understood it had become pitch black. Countless plays used this for comic effect – something Peter Shaffer rediscovered for modern audiences in his *Black Comedy.*

The whole arrangement of the stage was both simple and immensely flexible. Its great strength was that it packed a huge number of people into a small enough space in such a way as to allow an extraordinary concentration of audience attention on the stage. And stage and audience were close enough together to allow a powerfully close relationship between actor and audience.

In this play especially, the main audience focus would be on the actors. The play functions both as an awesome test for the actors' skills: and a fantastic opportunity to put them on display.

The Actors

In one of his plays, *Pedro de Urdemalas*, Cervantes makes it clear that what audiences expected from actors then were in some respects very similar to what we expect now: the ability to put expression in voice, face and body that matched the emotion of the lines.

They also needed an amazing memory – rehearsal times were short, and there were often hundreds of lines to master in a very short time – as well as physical stamina, voice control, and that rare combination of intellectual, musical and intellectual skills involved in the successful delivery of verse. It was said that their skills of diction and gesture were so extraordinary that often preachers would go to the theatre to pick up tips on the best way to deliver sermons.

Actors would also need something almost impossible to teach: a stage presence of sufficient authority to control the notoriously restive and demanding audience. A visit to the reconstruction of Shakespeare's Globe on London's South Bank will give today's audiences some indication of the qualities needed by actors working in these conditions – and some feeling for the overall conditions in which Calderón's public plays were first performed.

The actors would also need to be equally at home in comedy and tragedy, in allegorical drama and palace spectacle, to be able to dance, and to be able to sing.

It was a skilled trade, one usually passed down in families; and a trade whose skill was recognised and celebrated. An actor delivering a long speech with bravura and skill would expect a round of applause – just like an opera singer now at the end of a spectacularly difficult aria.

An important difference between actors then and now is in the way theatre companies were structured. Contracts were generally signed in Lent, when there was no theatrical activity at all, and the actor would sign on a for a whole season. The contracts specified very precisely the actor's particular role in a rigidly hierarchical structure.

The companies were led by the *autor de comedias* (director), who would direct and choose the plays, and also play the leading roles. He would also choose the actors to fill all the vacant slots in the hierarchy:

1st *galán* (leading man: in this play, Segismundo)

2nd *galán* (Astolfo)

1st *dama* (leading lady: Rosaura)

2nd *dama* (Estrella)

1st *barba* (old man, or king: Basilio)

2nd *barba* (Clotaldo)

Gracioso (comedian: Clarín)

Completing the company, there would probably be two more actors, one more actress, three musicians, a prompter (who'd be in charge of the scripts), a *guardarropa* (in charge of wardrobe and props), and someone to look after the accounts.

As actors grew older they might move up (or down) the hierarchy, from 2nd *dama* to first, say, or from *galán* to *barba*. But essentially they would take the same role over and over again, albeit in a string of different plays; and so the public would associate them exclusively with that role.

This is not completely foreign to us; when we think of Sean Connery for instance, we think of James Bond. And then if we see Pierce Brosnan in the same role, we tend to measure him up in relation to his predecessor.

The comedian, in particular, would over the years develop a strong stage personality which would be a given factor in every role he took on. It is almost certain that whoever took the role in the play's first performance would have used it as a framework for improvised comic business of his own. Which is one reason why the part of Clarín seems so undeveloped as a character.

Where Calderón could innovate was in the use he made of the role: Clarín's death, and the words he speaks on dying would have enormous impact in their original performance simply because the comedian did not normally get killed off in the course of the story.

It's as if actors, playwright and public were playing a game whose rules they all knew inside out. So the audience has a stake in the play, an informed knowledge of it that enables them to make it their own. In much the same way, television audiences today know the unwritten 'rules' governing the format and characters of certain drama series and 'soaps'. This expert shared knowledge empowers them to make the dramas part of their own lives; and endlessly discuss the twists and turns of their plots.

Just as a master chess player can take a limited set of pieces and moves to construct an infinite variety of games, so the playwright then can manipulate his chess pieces, his roles, to create for the audience an entertainment which possesses both the reassurance of a familiar and ordered world and the stimulus of the new and unexpected.

The World of the Play

For us, however, approaching this play in a totally different setting, things are perhaps not quite so easy. Perhaps it's useful to reflect on the implications of its title.

For when we have a dream, we just accept it at the time. Amazing things happen, and we just let ourselves be amazed. It's only afterwards that, if we choose, we can think about what happened in our dream and sometimes find ways of relating it to what is happening in our lives.

It is the same with this play: the weirdest things happen. There's a father so afraid of the power of his son that he locks him up in a tower the minute he is born. There's a man who falls asleep in a prison and wakes up in a palace. He doesn't know whether he's awake or still dreaming and throws someone out of a window to try to find out. There's a woman who's so angry with her lover for cheating on her that she dresses as a man and rides all the way from Moscow to Poland just to try to get even with him . . .

And all these extraordinary events add up to something that's funny, exciting, moving and strange . . . and when we think about them afterwards maybe we'll find that they have something to say about the way parents treat their children, or the way men and women relate together, or the extent to which we are really able to control the events of our lives.

No doubt the audience of the time would have been reflecting on the extraordinary problems of succession that kept afflicting their own royal family; or the apparent inability of their government to control events. No doubt the king himself, if he were watching, would be led to reflect on the extent to which his power was no more than an illusion.

Basilio is a king who tries to foretell and influence events. As I write, presidents and prime ministers gather for yet another world summit: with their bodyguards and their limousines they present an imposing spectacle. But the spectacle of power is an illusion, a dream.

Indonesia is in the throes of revolution, and India has just exploded an atomic bomb. Just like Basilio they have to confront events of huge importance: events that for all their wisdom and intelligence services they were unable to foretell. And certainly now have only the most limited ability to influence.

No doubt when Calderón wrote the scenes between Basilio and Segismundo he was reflecting on the troubled and stormy relationship with his own father; in a literal sense none of us has spent a childhood imprisoned in a tower. But the tower can as well function as a metaphor for the value systems of beliefs our parents tried to impose on us; and that we, in our turn, may be trying to impose on our children.

The tower imprisons us, but also guarantees a certain safety. Like Segismundo, all of us have to break out of it and try to determine what is truly valuable and what is not in the world outside. We need to learn to distinguish between what really matters and what is as insubstantial and as apparently unimportant as a dream.

A Note on the Translation

This translation was prepared for performance at the 1998 Edinburgh International Festival but was printed here before the performances took place. As such it feels very much like a work in progress: and a work whose outcome I find impossible to predict.

It has been partly prepared in collaboration with the director, Calixto Bieito, who introduced me to the work of José M. Ruano de la Haza on the text.

His work *La primera versión de 'La vida es sueño' de Calderón* (Liverpool 1992) proves that a hitherto largely overlooked early edition of the play represents an earlier version, subsequently reworked by Calderón for inclusion in his *Primera parte de comedias* (first published volume of plays).

It is very clear that this primitive version is closer to the play's first performance; some of its more outstanding lines have been incorporated into this translation.

For Further Reading

There is very little available in English that does not presuppose a knowledge of Spanish. Gwynne Edwards' book is an introduction to Calderón; the others contain useful information about theatre of the time.

Gwynne Edwards, *The Prison and the Labyrinth* (Cardiff 1978)

Malveena McKendrick, *Theatre in Spain 1490–1700* (Cambridge 1989)

A.A. Parker, *The Approach to the Spanish Drama of the Golden Age* (London 1957)

N.D. Shergold, *A History of the Spanish Stage*, Oxford 1967

Calderon: Key Dates

To Ferdy Woodward
with gratitude

LIFE IS A DREAM

Characters

ROSAURA   *(lady)*

CLARIN   *(comedian)*

SEGISMUNDO   *(prince)*

CLOTALDO   *(old man)*

ASTOLFO   *(prince)*

ESTRELLA   *(princess)*

BASILIO   *(king)*

GUARD 1/SOLDIER 1/COURTIER 1

MUSICIANS

ACT ONE

A noise off. ROSAURA *falls onto the stage. She is dressed as a man.*

ROSAURA. Call yourself a horse! You hippogriff!
    Violently running, fast as the wind,
    Then falling like a meteor crashing
    Into the labyrinth, into the maze,
    Of these naked mountain crags.
    You're a thunderbolt with a limp!
    A bird without wings. A fish without scales.
    Stay in this mountain. You be its Phaeton
    You be so foolish and fall from the sky!
    Abandon me! Leave me here, desperate, alone
    With no map or path to guide me
    Nothing but the working of blind chance
    As I struggle randomly through the tangled hair
    On the head of this giant mountain.
    Whose furrowed ridges frown at the sun.
    And this is Poland! You vile country!
    Viciously greeting this stranger
    Writing your greeting in letters of blood.
    I've hardly arrived. Such a hard arrival.
    Where can I find pity in my pitiless fate
    Arriving in anguish. Greeted with hate.

    Enter CLARIN.

CLARIN. Wait a minute. 'Where can I find pity?'
What about me? Why not 'Where can we . . . '
Where can we find pity? That's a better line.
After all, it was the two of us left home,
Looking for adventure, us two,
Sadly and madly reaching this god forsaken place.
Us two rolling half way down this mountain
Us two sharing disaster and pain
So it's us two who get to complain.

ROSAURA. Listen, Clarin, I didn't mention you in my
       speech
Because I didn't want to deprive you of your opportunity
To make your own. To lament your misfortune,
Find consolation in your grief. Remember the philosopher
Who said that to complain was such a pleasure
That misfortunes should be looked for, like a moral treasure.

CLARIN. Lady, your philosopher's an idiot and I wish
       he was here
So I could kick his head in. Only then I'd have to
       hear him
Complaining about my utterly amazing skill in kicking.
But, lady, look at us. Look at the state we're in.
On foot, completely and utterly lost
In a totally deserted mountain
With night falling like a guillotine.
Even the sun's deserting us.
We're completely on our own.

ROSAURA. Is there anyone who's ever seen anything
So utterly extraordinary and strange?
And it could be my eyes are deceiving me

Or my imagination's playing tricks on my fearful mind
But in the faint cold light of the dying day
I think I can see a building.

CLARIN. That's what I want to see
And if it turns out not to be actually there
I'll destroy the scenery.

ROSAURA. The mountains are so high
And the building is so low
It's as if the sun's hardly able to see it.
Its construction is so crude
It could be one of the rocks that surround it
Rocks casting such fierce shadows
It's as if they hurt the sunlight.

CLARIN. Lady, I think we're talking too much here,
Why don't we get a little closer
So that the kind people who live round here
Can welcome us with food and wine
And let us sit by a roaring fire to warm ourselves?

ROSAURA. The door – no. I could put that better –
        this black mouth . . .
Its sinister jaws yawn open, and the dark night within
Engenders a deeper darkness.

Chains sound inside.

CLARIN. Good grief what's that?

ROSAURA. I cannot move. I'm a block of fire and ice.
Burning with curiosity. Frozen with fear.

CLARIN. It's just someone been to the loo
And is pulling at the chain.

SEGISMUNDO (*within*)
    All I know of life is pain!

ROSAURA. What sadness in that voice. What desperation!
    I'm left struggling with new grief and pain.

CLARIN. Me with new fear.

ROSAURA. Clarin!

CLARIN. My lady!

ROSAURA. Let's run from the terrors
    Of this evil and enchanted tower.

CLARIN. Lady, when it comes down to it,
    I'm too petrified to even run.

ROSAURA. Is that a light, that feeble exhalation,
    That pale and trembling star,
    That pulse so weakly beating
    In so obscure and dubious a dwelling
    That, far from lightening,
    Appears to darken it.
    In its dim light I can barely see
    A dark prison lit by a single flame
    The burial place of a living corpse.
    And as if that were not amazing enough
    There's a man chained like an animal
    A lonely man with one small light.

SEGISMUNDO *is discovered. He is dressed in animal skins, with a chain on his leg, in such a way that he can get up and walk when his cue comes. He speaks the whole speech sitting on the ground.*

SEGISMUNDO. All I know of life is pain
    And I don't understand

Why I must live like this.
What crime did I commit?
The worst thing I do is to exist.
When I think of that I understand
A human's greatest crime is to be born!
But there's still something to be explained
The bitter dregs left to be drained.
And I still don't really understand
I must have done something else
For life to treat me like this.
Aren't other beings born?
What privilege is it they possess?
And what is it I so badly lack?
When a bird is born, it is so beautiful
Its feathers like the petals of a flower
It can barely fly before it leaves
The kind safety of its parents nest
And then it's gliding, freely gliding
Through the vast halls of the empty sky.
I have more soul than a bird
Why should I have less liberty?
When a beast is born, its skin becomes
A mirror of the patterns of the stars.
It can barely walk before human need
Stalks it, captures it, teaches it cruelty:
And then it's hunting with vicious greed
Through the endless tunnels of nature's maze.
I have more feeling than a brute,
Why should I have less liberty?
When a fish is born, it does not breathe,
It's an abortion of mud and slime.
It can barely swim before it glides

Like a ship of fins and scales
And then it's sailing in immensity
Through the vast cold heart of the endless sea.
I have more freewill than a fish
Why should I have less liberty?
When a stream is born, it's like a snake
Uncoiling its length past rocks and flowers
Like a silver serpent it begins to glide
And its waters sing as they break on the stones,
Celebrating the kindness of the life-giving sky.
I have more life than a stream
Why should I have less liberty?
And when I reach this moment
My heart burns like a volcano.
I want to tear it from my chest
And rip it into pieces!
How can it be justified
And how can it be right
For God to give freedom
– Sweet and beautiful freedom –
To give it to a stream, a fish,
A brute and a bird
And deny it to a human being!

ROSAURA. Your words fill me with pity and fear.

SEGISMUNDO. Who was it heard me?
Was it Clotaldo?

CLARIN. Say yes.

ROSAURA. No. It was a lonely cry of grief
Lost in these cold vaults of stone
Feeling for your sadness.

SEGISMUNDO *grabs her.*

SEGISMUNDO. Then I'll kill you.
    I can't have you knowing
    I know you know my weakness.
    Just because you heard me weep
    These strong arms of mine
    Will tear you into pieces.

CLARIN. I'm stone deaf. I never heard a word.

ROSAURA. You were born a human being.
    It will be enough to touch your heart
    Enough to fall helpless at your feet
    For you to free me.

SEGISMUNDO. Your voice could fill me with tenderness
    Your presence could fill me with . . . what?
    I hesitate; I look at you with . . . awe.
    Who are you? I know so little of the world.
    This tower is my cradle and my grave.
    Since the day I was born,
    If this is really what it is to live,
    All I've known is this desert place,
    This bare mountain, where I live in misery
    Like a skeleton which walks
    Like a corpse which breathes.
    There's only one man I've ever spoken to or seen.
    He feels for me in my misfortune.
    He brings me news of earth and heaven.
    Be amazed at me, call me a monster,
    I'm an animal, and I am a man.
    I am a man, and I'm an animal.
    Amidst all this misfortune, all this grief

Even though I've studied politics
Just by observing the wild beasts
And being taught by the flight of birds,
And though I've measured the perfect circles
Of the motions of the harmonious stars,
I've never seen in anyone
The perfect beauty that I see in you.
What force and what authority
Do you possess since you….
You, you alone have caused to halt
My fury at my wrongs
And filled my ears with pity?
Each time I look at you you amaze me more.
The more I look at you
The more I want to see you again and again.
My eyes must have a kind of rabies
For even when it's death to drink
They want to drink in more and more
And even though I understand
That seeing is a kind of death
I am still dying to see more.

ROSAURA. It so moves me to hear you
It amazes me to see you
And I don't know what to say to you
And I don't know what to ask you.
All I'll say is that somehow fate
Must have guided me here to find comfort,
If anyone unhappy really can be comforted
In seeing someone more unhappy still.
I know a story of a wise philosopher
Who was so deeply sunk in poverty

That all he could find to eat
Were wild herbs he picked off the roadside.
Can there possibly be anyone, he wondered,
Who's as poor and as wretched as me?
And then he looked back, and then he saw
Another wise philosopher
Eating the leaves that he had thrown away.
And there I was, full of self-pity
Wondering if there could be anyone
So miserable and wretched as I.
And you have given me your sad reply.
For after listening to your story
I find my griefs have disappeared.
You have gathered them, and turned them into happiness.
Perhaps my misfortunes can help relieve your pain.
So I'll tell my story. Take from it
All my superfluous grief. I am –

CLOTALDO. Guards of this tower,
    Are you cowards?
    Are you asleep?
    Two intruders
    Have broken into the tower!

ROSAURA. Now new confusion fills me.

SEGISMUNDO. That is Clotaldo, my jailer.
    There is still no end to all my sufferings.

CLOTALDO. Stir yourselves! Capture or kill them
    Before they can defend themselves!

CLARIN. Guards of the tower,
    Just remember he's offering you a choice

You can capture us or kill us.
Capturing is so much easier.

Enter CLOTALDO *and* SOLDIERS.

CLOTALDO. Hide your faces. No-one should know us.

CLARIN. Ooh it's a masked ball.

CLOTALDO. Ignorant fools, you've trespassed
On forbidden ground, broken the king's decree
Which forbids anyone to view or see
This dangerous monster imprisoned here.
Surrender: or this gun, like a metal cobra,
Will spit two balls of poisoned fire
Through the terrified and frozen air.

SEGISMUNDO. You monster of injustice,
I'll die before I see you touch
Or harm them, I'll tear myself to pieces
With these chains, these rocks,
With my own teeth before I consent
To their suffering or weep for their pain!

CLOTALDO. God decreed, Segismundo, you should die
Before you were even born. That's how monstrous
Are your misfortunes. You know that.
And you also know you need these chains
To hold back the proud fury of your rage.
So why make idle boasts? Take him back
To his cell: lock him in. Hide him
From our sight.

SEGISMUNDO.   God in heaven
How wise you are to deprive me
Of my freedom! For otherwise

I'd tear down the mountains
To build a ladder of stone.
I'd climb up to attack the sky!
I'd be a giant and destroy the sun
And I'd smash heaven's crystal spheres!

They overpower SEGISMUNDO *and lock him back in his cell.*

CLOTALDO. Perhaps it's to prevent you
That you suffer such misfortune.

ROSAURA. Obviously pride offends you. I'll try humility,
Fall at your feet, and beg for my life.
It would be remarkable cruelty
If humbleness offended you as much as pride.

CLARIN. I don't expect you to be impressed by either.
Humility and pride are both unbelievably dull,
And besides they've both had parts
In endless allegorical dramas. So I won't be humble,
And I won't be proud. I'm kind of in between the two
And ask you nicely to be kind.

CLOTALDO. You!

GUARD. My lord!

CLOTALDO. Take their weapons and blindfold their eyes.

ROSAURA. This is my sword. It can only be given to you,
For you are the noblest here, and it will refuse
To be taken by anyone of less nobility.

CLARIN. My sword isn't fussy. Any shit can have it.
You take it.

ROSAURA. All I ask is that you take good care of it
For the sake of the man who once wore it.

When CLOTALDO *takes* ROSAURA'*s sword, he is
disturbed.*

CLOTALDO (*aside*). (God help me, I know this sword.
  Holding it fills my heart with pain.
  And it's hard to believe that this is true
  And not part of some appalling dream.)
  Who are you?

ROSAURA.   A stranger.

CLOTALDO. Obviously, since you did not know
  This place was forbidden you.

ROSAURA. Even if I had known it, there was nothing I could
  do.
  This mad horse of mine tried to be some kind of bird,
  Threw me off its back and left me stranded in
  misfortune.

CLOTALDO. Where you from?

ROSAURA   Moscow.

CLOTALDO.   I have many ties
  With that nation. Why have you come?

ROSAURA. I have been insulted. I lost my self-respect.
  I have come to seek revenge.

CLOTALDO.   (Oh God
  Each new moment adds to my unhappiness.)

ROSAURA. And so I beg you, keep this sword safe; for if
  By any freak of chance I am spared this sentence
  And allowed to live, then this sword will regain
  My honour; for although I do not understand
  What secret this sword contains, I know

It holds one. Though it could well be
That I deceive myself, and only value it
Because it is the only object I possess
That was once my father's.

CLOTALDO.   Who was he?

ROSAURA. I never knew him.

CLOTALDO.   How do you know
    This sword contains a secret?

ROSAURA. The one who gave it me said: 'Go to Poland
    Be secret, careful, skilful, and make sure
    The leaders there see you with this sword.
    For I know that one of them will show you favour
    And will safeguard you. Or will, if he still lives.
    But for now, in case he's dead,
    I'll hide his name in silence.'

CLOTALDO. (My heart like a prisoner hammers
    At the bars of its cell. Like a moth,
    It beats its wings. It flies up
    To the window to look out in the street.
    And so I feel tears in my eyes
    Weeping at the window of my soul.
    I gave this sword to my lover,
    The beautiful Violante, and I told her
    Anyone who wore it would find me
    A kind and loving father to my own son.
    But I don't know what favour or help
    I can give him, when I'm supposed to drive
    The sword's point into his chest.
    What can I do? What can I do?
    If I take him to the king

I am taking him to die.
But that is what my duty commands.
My hands are tied by duty,
My heart is driven by love.
But I should be in no doubt.
They say that loyalty to the king
Matters more than honour, more
Than life itself. So let duty live,
Let love die. They also say
That anyone who has lost their honour
And their self respect cannot be noble.
He tells me he's my son. It cannot be true.
He cannot have my noble blood.
But all that's happened to him is a danger
No-one can escape, because honour
Is so fragile, it's broken with a single blow.
It's shattered by a breath of wind.
And he, with anger and with courage,
Is seeking revenge. What else can anyone do?
He is my son, his boldness proves it.
What can I do? Take courage!
The best thing is to take him to the king,
Tell him he's my son and should be killed.
Perhaps the extreme loyalty I'll show him
Will oblige him to show mercy; if not,
If the king is constant in his cruelty, then the boy
Will die without knowing he is my son.)
Foreigners, come this way, and don't imagine
You're alone in your misfortunes.
In dilemmas like these it's hard to tell
Which is the greater misfortune: to die or live.

Exit.

A sound of trumpets and drums; enter, on one side, ASTOLFO *accompanied by* SOLDIERS, *and* ESTRELLA *on the other accompanied by* WOMEN.

ASTOLFO. Your eyes are like comets, madam.
    They announce the death of kings.
    Your exquisite beauty inspires these trumpets.
    To greet you they become metal birds.
    Their mouthpieces sprout feathers
    And fly through the air. Cannons salute you
    As empress; the palace fountains greet you
    As the goddess of spring; the trumpets
    Greet you as the goddess of war, and the birds
    Greet you as the goddess of dawn.
    Day has come to send the night to exile
    But you are more radiant still
    In joyfulness you are the dawn
    In beauty you are the spring
    In anger you are war itself
    And you are the ruler of my soul.

ESTRELLA. What we say must correspond
    With what we do. I think it wrong
    For you to flatter me in such courteous terms
    When your words are so plainly contradicted
    By your obvious preparations for war.
    I'm not afraid to fight against them, Prince,
    For the flatteries I hear do not correspond
    To the hostility I see before me. Remember,
    Prince, how vile it is to flatter with the tongue,
    But kill with the intention.

ASTOLFO. Estrella you are ill-informed
   If you doubt that I'm sincere
   In praising you. I beg you listen.
   When the last king of Poland died
   He left two daughters and his son
   Basilio to inherit the throne.
   Your mother was the eldest daughter,
   Mine the youngest. She married in Moscow,
   Of whose state I am now Prince.
   As for Basilio, he is the victim
   Of advancing old age; and he has always cared
   More for his studies than for women or vice.
   Since he is childless, we are both entitled to inherit:
   You as the offspring of the elder child,
   And myself because I am a man.
   We told our uncle of our competing claims
   And he promised to meet us here, today,
   And satisfy us both. That is why I left Moscow,
   That is why I came here; not to make war on you
   But so you could lay loving siege to my heart.
   Dear princess, I pray the god of love be wise
   And that the common people, the only true astrologer,
   May bless this union and crown you queen
   – Queen, that is, of my tender heart.

ESTRELLA. Such extraordinary courtesy is exactly
   What my high rank deserves, and of course
   It would be the most enormous pleasure
   For me to gain the imperial crown,
   Solely to hand it over to you.
   But I know you have come here to deceive me
   Because the flattery of your words

Is undermined by the girl
Whose portrait you wear round your neck.

A drum beats.

ASTOLFO. How greatly I regret that sound
For it prevents me explaining
And proclaims the arrival of the King!

Drums beat. Enter KING BASILIO, *an old man, and his court.*

ESTRELLA. Allow me to tenderly embrace

ASTOLFO. Allow me to tenderly entwine

ESTRELLA. My arms around your feet in humble coils.

ASTOLFO. My arms like ivy round your majestic trunk.

BASILIO. Nephew, niece, embrace me. I know you
    love me,
Because you have faithfully obeyed
My loving request with such kind words
And I want to leave neither unsatisfied
And both of you on equal terms.
You know my knowledge has earned me
The title of Basilio the wise.
The sciences I love the most
And engage in with a subtle and discerning mind
Are those which foretell the future,
Which steal the function of passing time
To tell us what happens with each day that comes.
For I can look at astrological tables
And I can foresee the future in the present.
The planets revolve in circles of snow
The stars spread out a canopy of diamonds

These are the subjects of my studies,
The sky is like a book to me, a book
Of diamond paper, with sapphire binding,
Written in letters of gold, hieroglyphics
I can read and easily decipher. And so I know
What the future holds for each of us, for good or bad.
But I wish to God that my own life
Had been the first target of the heaven's anger,
Long before I learnt to interpret its messages
And learnt to understand its signs.
For when a man is unfortunate
Even his gifts stab him in the back
And a man whose knowledge harms him
Murders his own self! This I can tell you,
Though in the events of my sad life
It is still better told. So once again
It is for silence that I ask you.
Clorilene my wife gave birth to a son.
The omens of his birth were so many, and so dreadful
They exhausted the skies. While the baby still lay
In the womb's living grave, far from the beautiful light
Of day, she dreamt again and again of her belly torn open
By a monster in the shape of a man.
And on the day that he was born, the sun itself
Engaged in blood-soaked battle with the moon
With the earth as the battlefield. This was the worst eclipse
The world has suffered since weeping for the death
     of Christ.
The sun was smothered in living fire,
The heavens darkened, palaces trembled,
The clouds rained stones and the rivers ran with
     torrents of blood.

And it was under this sign
My son Segismundo was born.
He foretold his future in the manner of his birth,
For in being born he killed his mother
And so boasted with male ferocity:
'Look: I am human and this how
We humans repay those who do us good.'
I ran to my books, and in them I read
Segismundo would be the most brutal man,
The cruellest prince, the most vicious monarch.
That under him his kingdom would become
Divided, split, torn by civil wars:
I saw him inspired by fury.
I saw him driven on by rage.
I saw him defeat and overcome me.
I saw me lying vanquished at his feet.
I saw me humiliated, helpless,
And forced to be his wretched slave.
His feet – and how it shames me to confess it –
Would make a carpet out of my white hairs.
Self love plays such a part in science
And when despite of it science predicts
So dire an outcome, we must believe it.
We know that evil is far more likely to occur than good
And good endings are never as plausible as bad.
I had to believe such frightening predictions
I had to try to avert the evil that seemed sure to come.
I had to see if wisdom can help a human overcome
    the stars.
So I prepared a tower, hidden in the mountains,
Where the daylight scarcely dares enter.
I passed strict laws and edicts,

I forbade anyone to enter
And I had it announced that the prince was born dead.
There Segismundo lives, chained like a beast,
Imprisoned in poverty and misery.
Only Clotaldo has spoken to him and seen him;
He has taught him divine law and human knowledge
And been the only witness of his unhappy life.
Three things must be considered here. The first
That I love my country, and I must do all I can
To rescue it from the prospect of a cruel vindictive king.
The second is that we are talking of my son.
He has the right to freedom, he has the right to rule.
To deprive him of these rights would be a crime,
A crime I cannot justify,
Even if what I intend is the good of all.
The third is that we know we should not too easily
    believe
That what is predicted will unavoidably occur.
Even the most evil omen, even the worst horoscope
Can only incline the will. It cannot force it.
And so my friends you must imagine me
Struggling for many months with these dilemmas
Until today, when I have finally found
A solution that will utterly amaze you.
Tomorrow I will place my son on the throne
I will not tell him that he is my son, or that he is
    your king
But he will govern you, and you will swear obedience.
Now think what that this achieves.
It resolves the three issues I have set before you.
One: I love my country, and if I give you a king
Who rules with justice, wisdom and goodwill

Then the stars' predictions are defeated, and you enjoy
The government of your rightful king.
Second: I will not commit a crime
Because if he acts unjustly, cruelly,
Gives free rein to viciousness and vice
Then I can depose him and imprison him again
And that will not be cruelty but just punishment.
Third, if the horoscope is right it can all still be remedied
If I marry Estrella to Astolfo, set them on the throne
And give you rulers who will be worthy of the task.
This I command you as your king
This I ask you as a father,
This I request you as a philosopher
And if what Seneca said is really true,
And the king really is the slave of his own kingdom
Then this I humbly beg you as your slave.

ASTOLFO. It is my duty to reply to this
As the one whose interests are most at stake
In the name of all I say:
Bring us Segismundo, for he is your son.
And that is enough for all of us.

ALL. Give us our Prince
for we ask him to be our king!

BASILIO. Vassals, I respect and thank you
For this generous act. Accompany
These two pillars of the state to their rooms
For tomorrow you will see him.

ALL. Long live the great king Basilio!

Exit all. Before the KING *exits,* CLOTALDO *enters with*
ROSAURA *and* CLARIN *and stops the* KING.

CLOTALDO. Can I speak to you?

BASILIO. Oh Clotaldo, you are most welcome!

CLOTALDO. Coming into your presence, majesty,
    Always fills me with joy, but today
    An angry twist of vicious destiny
    Has robbed a law of its privilege
    And a custom of its joy.

BASILIO. What troubles you?

CLOTALDO. A misfortune, your majesty, has occurred;
    Although it should have been a source of joy.

BASILIO. Go on.

CLOTALDO.   This young man, your majesty,
    And it is hard to repress my tears
    He entered the tower, and saw the prince.
    And he is –

BASILIO.   Do not trouble yourself Clotaldo.
    Even if this happened through carelessness
    You have no need to excuse it
    I have just revealed the secret
    And it does not matter he should know it.
    See me afterwards, because I have much to tell you
    And there is much for you to do for me;
    For I must tell you you are to be the instrument
    Of the most amazing event the world has ever seen.
    As for these prisoners, so that you know
    I do not punish in them your carelessness
    I forgive them. Let them go.

Exit BASILIO.

CLOTALDO. Great king, may you live a thousand centuries!
  (My poor heart, the first ordeal is over.
  Now let the next ordeal begin.)
  Foreign travellers, you are free.

ROSAURA. I kiss your feet a thousand times.

CLARIN. I'll make do with a couple of hundred.
  A few kisses more or less
  Won't matter between friends.

ROSAURA. My lord, you have given me my life.
  I will for ever be your grateful slave.

CLOTALDO. You're wrong. I never gave you life.

ROSAURA. Why not?

CLOTALDO. A man of noble birth who's been dishonoured
  Does not truly live. And since you have come
  To avenge an insult, that obviously applies to you.
  I could not have given you life
  For living in dishonour is no life at all.
  (I hope that I encourage him to speak.)

ROSAURA. I admit for now I have no proper life
  Even though I receive it from you.
  But when I take my revenge
  I will regain my self-respect.
  My life then without any doubt at all
  Will seem like a gift from you.

CLOTALDO. Don't go without a weapon.
  Take this sword you brought
  For I know it will suffice for your revenge
  And will be stained with your enemy's blood;

For this blade will know how to revenge you
I know, for it once was mine – or rather,
Mine for this instant, for this brief time
I have held it in my power.

ROSAURA. And so for the second time in your name
I put on this sword and swear to obtain revenge
However powerful my enemy may be.

CLOTALDO. And is he?

ROSAURA. So powerful, I will not disclose his name;
For I would not wish to lose your friendship.

CLOTALDO. But if you were to tell me
It would strengthen my concern for you,
For it would make it impossible
For me to help your enemy.
(Oh I wish I knew who it was.)

ROSAURA. So you do not think I place a low value on
    the trust
You place in me, you must know my enemy
Is no less than Astolfo, the duke of Moscow.

CLOTALDO. (It's hard not to be overcome by grief.
The affair is far worse than I imagined.
Let's investigate a little further.)
If you were born a Muscovite
Then your natural lord could not insult you
Even if (anxiety will drive me mad!)
He called you a liar in public.

ROSAURA. I know that even though he was my prince
He could still offend me.

CLOTALDO. He could not, even though he slapped you
    in the face.
    (My God!)

ROSAURA. What I suffered was far worse!

CLOTALDO. Then tell it now, because you cannot say
    more
    Than what I already imagine.

ROSAURA. I look at you with a respect I do not
    understand.
    I look on to you with such deep regard,
    And I hold you in such great esteem,
    That I hardly dare tell you
    That how I appear is a disguise,
    That I am not whom I appear to be.
    Be alert; reflect;
    If I am not who I seem
    And Astolfo came here to marry Estrella,
    Think how he could offend me.
    I have already said too much.

    Exit ROSAURA *and* CLARIN.

CLOTALDO. Stop wait come back!
    What tangled labyrinth is this
    Where reason cannot find the thread?
    My honour is offended;
    The enemy is powerful;
    I am his vassal; she is my daughter.
    May heaven find some solution
    Although I doubt it can
    In so deep a pit of confusion

The whole sky is an omen
The whole world a prodigious portent.

Exit.

End of Act One.

ACT TWO

CLOTALDO. Everything you ordered
  Has been accomplished.

BASILIO. Tell me what happened.

CLOTALDO. This is how it was.
  You ordered me to make a tranquillising drink,
  A drink made of herbs whose secret power
  Is to deprive a man of reason, to rob
  And dispossess him of awareness and of conscious will.
  In short: transform him to a living corpse.
  We don't need to convince anyone this is possible;
  For medicine, your majesty, is full of natural secrets;
  There is no animal, no plant, no stone
  That does not possess its own determined quality.
  And if we start to examine the thousand poisons
  Human malice uses to give death,
  It should come as no surprise to find
  That since there are poisons that can kill
  Once their destructive power is diluted,
  They should also bring sleep.
  Still, your majesty, leaving aside this fascinating question,
  Of whether it is possible for such a thing to occur
  – Since it is already proved by reason and empirical
    evidence –
  I went down to Segismundo with the drink

In which were mixed opium, henbane and belladona,
And there, in his small cell, I spoke to him
Of the human knowledge taught him by dumb nature,
Nature his mother, who in these learned solitudes
Has taught him the politics of the beasts and birds.
In order to elevate his spirits for your enterprise
I allowed him to see a royal eagle's soaring flight
Despising the sphere of the wind and rising
To the highest regions of fire, where it flew
Like a bright comet or a feathered lightning bolt.
I praised its proud flight, saying: 'In the end
You are king of the birds, and so it is right
That you should fly high above them all.'
That was enough; for when he thinks of kingship,
He thinks with ambition and with pride
– For he has a kind of blood in him
That inspires, moves, and spurs him on to great things –
And he said: 'To think that even in the unquiet republic
   of birds
There should be one to whom they swear obedience!'
When I saw how this occupied his mind
And it is the constant theme of his suffering.
I toasted him with the potion, and hardly
Had the liquid passed from glass to stomach
When he surrendered his strength to the power of sleep.
A cold sweat ran down through his veins and limbs,
So cold, that if I had not known this was pretended
   death,
I would have feared for his life.
At that moment the people came
In whom you have entrusted
The secret of this experiment.

They carried him to a coach, and then to your room
Where is prepared the greatness and majesty
Merited by his position. There they put him to bed
And there, once the drowsiness has lost its power,
There they will serve him as they would serve you,
Just as you ordered. And if having obeyed you in every
     respect
Makes me worthy of any slight reward
Then all I would ask you
– forgive my indiscretion –
Is that you tell me what you intend
In bringing Segismundo here to the palace.

BASILIO. Clotaldo, that is a very good question
     And to you alone will I answer it in full.
     You already know that the influence of the stars
     On my son Segismundo threatens us all
     With endless misfortunes and tragic events.
     It is impossible for the heavens to lie
     And they have given us so many proofs of their veracity –
     But I want to examine whether it is possible
     For the heavens to relent a little or mitigate their
          harshness
     Or to see whether with boldness and prudence
     They can be contradicted, whether human beings
     Have power over their own destiny.
     This is what I want to investigate,
     And this is why I have brought him here:
     So he may be told he is my son,
     And to have his ability put to the test.
     If he has the greatness of spirit to overcome himself,
     Then he will be king; but if he shows himself to be cruel,

Or indulges in the abuse of power,
I'll return him to his chains.
Now you're going to ask, why, to determine this,
Was it necessary to drug him first?
I want to satisfy you in every respect.
If he knew now today that he was my son,
And then tomorrow saw himself reduced again
To prison and to misery, it is certain that he would
Despair in his condition. For having known who he
   really is
What consolation could he possibly find?
I wanted to leave him a remedy for future misery
By telling him that everything he saw
Was no more than a dream. So this achieves two ends:
Firstly his disposition, since while he is awake
He behaves exactly as he imagines and thinks.
Secondly his consolation, because even though he sees
   himself
Obeyed now and then returned to his chains,
He could still believe he dreamt it all
And that will be a good understanding for him to have,
Because in this world, Clotaldo,
Everyone who lives is dreaming.

CLOTALDO. I can think of many reasons
   To demonstrate you are mistaken
   But now it is all too late
   For the signs are that he has woken,
   And he is coming this way.

BASILIO. I shall withdraw; you are his tutor,
   You go up to him. His mind will be full
   Of confusion. So tell him the truth.

CLOTALDO. You mean tell him who he is?

BASILIO. Yes; for it could be if he knows it
   He will recognise his danger
   And be more inclined to overcome himself.

   Exit BASILIO. *Enter* CLARIN.

CLARIN. Getting in here isn't cheap is it?
   This man standing at the door
   Wanted to see my ticket. I said
   You won't catch me buying one of those.
   The price they are nowadays
   Do you think I'm stupid?
   I don't need a ticket. I've got my eyes.
   Keep them wide open
   And you can see anything.

CLOTALDO. (O god, that's Clarin, the servant of that
      woman
   That dealer in misfortune
   Who has carried my shame into Poland.)
   Clarin, what's new?

CLARIN. What's new, sir, is that your enormous kindness
   Always so ready to avenge Rosaura's wrongs,
   Has advised her to dress as her own sex.

CLOTALDO. Of course. So as not to cause a scandal.

CLARIN. And what's also new sir is that she's changed
      her name,
   And is now known as your niece.

CLOTALDO. I'm taking responsibility for her reputation.
   What else?

CLARIN.   Now she's a lady in waiting for the
    Extraordinary Estrella, and she's waiting for you
    To find the time and place to achieve her revenge.

CLOTALDO. That's as it should be. For all these things
    Will be set right in time.

CLARIN. And the other thing, sir, is that she is living
    In luxury, she is being treated like a queen
    And is the favourite of the princess,
    Whereas I, her faithful companion and friend
    Am dying of hunger, and everyone forgets me
    And forgets that I'm Clarin, and that Clarin
    – For the benefit of the ignorant – means trumpet.
    It's from the Latin. Clarinus. Or clarion.
    As in call. Clarion call. And I could call
    The king, Astolfo, and Estrella, to tell them
    Just what is going on and just who your niece
    Really is and what she's hoping to do here.

CLOTALDO. I think I understand you, and I'm sure
    That we'll get on. You work for me,
    And here's an advance on your wages.

CLARIN. And here comes Segismundo.

Enter as many as can be afforded, dressing SEGISMUNDO, *who
is now wearing beautiful clothes. He is amazed by everything, and
walks around while the* MUSICIANS *sing*

SEGISMUNDO. God help me! What do I see?
    God help me! What do I touch!
    I look at it with wonder!
    I see it with amazement!
    Me in this beautiful palace!

Me wearing satin and silk!
Me surrounded by all these
Elegant looking servants!
Me waking up to find myself
In that gorgeous feather bed!
I can't be. I'm dreaming;
I know I'm awake.
Aren't I still Segismundo?
Look just tell me, God,
What's supposed to be going on!
I mean what could have happened
To me while I was fast asleep?
What is it that I'm seeing now?
Well, whatever it is, why should
That bother me? Why worry?
I'll just let myself be waited on
And then just see what happens.

SERVANT 1. He's so preoccupied.

SERVANT 2. After what's happened to him
    Who wouldn't be?

CLARIN. I wouldn't be. I'd be jumping for joy.

SERVANT 1. Go and talk to him.

SERVANT 2. Should they sing again?

SEGISMUNDO.   No,
    I don't want any more singing.

SERVANT 2. I just wanted to entertain you.
    You seem so preoccupied.

SEGISMUNDO.   No, I

Don't think music helps me, really.
All I like are brass bands.

CLOTALDO. Your Highness, Great Lord,
    Allow me to kiss your hand.
    I will be honoured to be the first
    To swear obedience to you as Lord.

SEGISMUNDO. (That's Clotaldo. What's he doing?
    Why's he being so polite?
    When I was in prison he treated me like a pig.
    What is happening to me?)

CLOTALDO. Your life has so suddenly changed
    And your heart and mind will be filled
    With confusion and doubts.
    And if I can, I want to help you understand.

He becomes grave.

Great lord, you have to understand
That you are Prince of Poland.
You will inherit the throne.
You've been hidden in a tower
Because the stars foretold
A most terrible tragedy
Would occur when you were crowned.
But if he makes use of the power
Of reason a good-hearted man
Can overcome the stars
We must trust that truth.
And that is why, while you were sleeping
You were taken from the tower
And brought to this palace.

My lord, the king your father,
Will come here soon and from him
You'll learn the rest.

SEGISMUNDO. You wicked foul betrayer
I've nothing else to learn.
I know all I need to know.
I've got pride now, I've got power
And I know you betrayed your country
Because you hid me and you denied me
My rightful place in the world!

CLOTALDO. (Oh no!)

SEGISMUNDO. You broke the law, you lied to the king
And you were cruel to me. And so
We all agree, the king, the law, and me
That you're condemned to death.
And I'm going to kill with these hands.

SERVANT 1. My lord!

SEGISMUNDO. Don't try to protect him. Don't waste your time
And listen, you, I swear to God,
If you get in my way
I'll chuck you out the window.

SERVANT 2. Clotaldo run!

CLOTALDO. You sad deluded fool, so savage in your pride
Without understanding that you're dreaming!

Exit CLOTALDO.

SERVANT 2. Just take note –

SEGISMUNDO. You keep out of this!

SERVANT 2. He was only obeying orders.

SEGISMUNDO. You shouldn't obey orders when they're
    wrong.
    And anyway I'm his prince.

SERVANT 2. But it wasn't up to him to think
    He just did what he was told.

SEGISMUNDO. So why don't you do the same?
    Instead of answering me back all the time!

CLARIN. Everything the Prince says is completely right
    And everything you say is completely wrong!

SERVANT 2. Who said you could speak like this?

CLARIN. I did.

SEGISMUNDO. Who are you?

CLARIN. I poke my nose into palaces.
    I step on official's toes.
    I destroy protocol.

SEGISMUNDO. In this strange new world
    You're the only one I like.

CLARIN. My lord, I'm the greatest Segismundo-pleaser
    In the whole wide world.

    Enter ASTOLFO.

ASTOLFO. Happy a thousand times this august day
    Dear prince, when you arrive to fill the world
    From west to east with joy and gladness.
    You rise like the sun from behind the savage mountains;

Rise then; and although the laurel wreath

He puts on his hat.

Is crowning your Imperial self a little late
May its freshness be as late in fading.

SEGISMUNDO. Morning.
   God keep you.

   He turns his back.

ASTOLFO. It's clear that you don't know me, and so
   I'll excuse you, this once, for not showing me more
      honour.
   My name is Astolfo, I'm by birth a Duke,
   And ruler of the principality of Moscow.
   From you I anticipate more respect.

SEGISMUNDO. I said 'God keep you'. Isn't God
   Good enough for you? Apparently not
   Since you're boasting about how important you are.
   Well next time we meet I'll ask God
   To shit on you instead!

SERVANT 2. Your Highness must bear in mind
   That he comes from the mountains
   And doesn't know any better.
   I'm sure, your grace, Astolfo would prefer . . .

SEGISMUNDO. It really annoyed me the way he just
      turned up
   And didn't bow to me. Instead he put his hat on.

SERVANT 2. He's a Great Man. He can do that.
   He's one of the Great and Good.

SEGISMUNDO. I'm greater. And I'm gooder.

SERVANT 2. Of course your grace, but none the less
　　It would be fitting for your relationships
　　To have a little more decorum –

SEGISMUNDO.　　　　　　　　　And
　　What's it got to do with you?

Enter ESTRELLA.

SEGISMUNDO. You there,
　　Come here, tell me, who is that?
　　That gorgeous woman, that divine beauty
　　Even the sun itself must bow down
　　To kiss her amazingly beautiful feet.

CLARIN. That's your cousin, lord. Her name's Estrella.
　　That means star.

SEGISMUNDO.　　What an appropriate name.

ESTRELLA. We are all of us eager to greet you, Highness,
　　And accept you as our king; and we hope
　　That in spite of difficulties, you are King
　　Not simply for years but for many centuries.

SEGISMUNDO. I thank you for making me welcome
　　But the best thing that's happened to me
　　Has been seeing you. I could forgive my father
　　If I'd had you in the mountain with me.
　　What could possibly be more cruel
　　Than deny a man the joy of seeing a woman?
　　Especially of seeing you, Estrella, you star
　　Whose rising puts the sun in the shade.

ESTRELLA. I think you should show a little more tact.

ASTOLFO. (If he says he loves her, then I am done for.)

SERVANT 2. (I understand Astolfo's trouble
And I want to set his mind at ease.)
My lord, you shouldn't say Estrella
Pleases you, because she's to marry
Astolfo –

SEGISMUNDO. Didn't I tell you to keep out my way?

SERVANT 2. Yes, but Astolfo's here –

SEGISMUNDO.   That's enough!

SERVANT 2. All I'm saying is what I know is right –

SEGISMUNDO. It can't be right if I don't like it!

SERVANT 2. But I thought I heard you tell me
The right thing was to do what you're told.

SEGISMUNDO. I thought I also told you
That anyone who angered me
Would be chucked out the nearest window!

SERVANT 2. But you can't do that to people like me.

SEGISMUNDO. Oh can't I? Let's find out!

He picks him up and exits with him, returning soon after.

ASTOLFO. What is happening?

ESTRELLA. Someone go and help him!

SEGISMUNDO. Thank you God it could be done.
He fell from the balcony into the sea.

ASTOLFO. Nonetheless you should take more care
And think before committing a cruelty.

A mountain is not the same as a palace.
A human is not the same as a beast.

SEGISMUNDO. Perhaps you should take more care as well
Or you'll find you don't have a head to put a hat on.

Exit ASTOLFO *and* ESTRELLA. *Enter the* KING.

BASILIO. What's happened?

SEGISMUNDO. Nothing. Someone made me angry.
I chucked him out the window.

CLARIN. Careful. This is the king.

SEGISMUNDO.   So what?

BASILIO. On your first day you kill a man!

SEGISMUNDO. He told me it couldn't be done.
So I proved him wrong.

BASILIO. It saddens me to see you
Acting with such cruelty.
I'm horrified your first action
Is to commit a cruel homicide.
I was hoping that you'd conquered destiny
And would be standing like an enlightened man
Triumphant over the prediction of the stars.
How can I come and embrace you now
When I know your hands are stained with blood
And that you have learnt the skill of murder?
Is there anyone here who wouldn't be afraid?
It's like seeing a dagger that's carried out a murder.
It's like seeing the spot where someone's been killed.
It makes you shiver. Self-preservation has to be
The strongest impulse. So when I look at your arms

I see a dagger, I see a place that's stained with blood,
And I recoil, disgusted. I was going to embrace you,
But now I turn my back, frightened and appalled.

SEGISMUNDO. Why should I care if you don't embrace
me?
I've had to live without it up to now,
With a father who brings me up with such cruelty
He locks me in a tower, treats me like an animal,
And tries to have me killed. Your embraces really
Do not count for much. What matters is
You stopped me being human!

BASILIO. I wish to God I'd never given you life
So I wouldn't have to hear your voice
Or feel your vile ingratitude.

SEGISMUNDO. If you'd never given me life I wouldn't
be complaining.
But you gave me life and then took it away from me.
Giving's the most amazing, noble act.
But to give and then to take away
That is the most contemptible.

BASILIO. You used to be a poor and helpless prisoner.
Now you're a rich and powerful prince.
Why don't you show some gratitude?

SEGISMUNDO. What have I to be grateful for?
You took away my freedom.
And now you're old and tired and dying
And all you're giving me is what is already mine.
You're my father, you're my king,
So although I'm now a prince

That's nothing to do with you.
That's the law of nature. I'm not
In debt to you, you're in debt to me!
You owe me all the years you took from me
When you stole my freedom and you stole my life!
Remember: You owe me. You be grateful.
Be grateful I don't make you pay.

BASILIO. You shameless barbarian. You proud, ignorant
    fool.
You're everything the stars predicted.
And even though you know who you are
And find yourself preferred above all
Remember this: you be humble, you be kind
Perhaps you're dreaming, as you'll find
When you wake up in your right mind.

Exit BASILIO.

SEGISMUNDO. I can't be dreaming. I can see and touch
All I have been and all I am.
And you may be sorry now for what you've done.
And you may sigh and sorely regret it.
But you are helpless because what you cannot take
From me is the fact I am prince and must inherit your
    throne.
And if once you saw me give up and accept my chains,
Despairing of the struggle,
That was because I didn't know who I was
But now my eyes are opened and I know who I am:
Half human half wild animal.

Enter ROSAURA, *dressed as a woman.*

ROSAURA (*aside*). (I've come in search of Estrella
  And I'm terrified of meeting Astolfo
  For Clotaldo wants him not to see me
  And not to know who I really am
  Clotaldo, to whom I owe this comfort,
  This safety, this soft life.)

CLARIN. Of all the things you've seen and admired
  What's the one that has pleased you most?

SEGISMUNDO. Nothing has amazed me at all;
  For I was ready for everything
  But if there's one thing I admire in this world
  It has to be woman's beauty. I read once,
  In one of the books I was given,
  That in the whole creation the one thing
  God worked the hardest to make was man,
  Because man is the whole world in miniature.
  But I think he must have worked harder creating woman
  Because women are much more beautiful,
  Women are a replica of heaven.
  Especially when she's the woman I see now.

ROSAURA (*aside*). (The prince is here; I must go back.)

SEGISMUNDO. Wait woman, stop! Don't run away.
  Don't be sunrise and sunset both at once.
  Night shouldn't come as soon as the sun rises
  Or the days would be unbearably short.
  (But who is this?)

ROSAURA. (I can't believe what I am seeing. Yet I must ...)

SEGISMUNDO. (I have seen this beauty somewhere else.)

ROSAURA. (I have seen this power in chains.)

SEGISMUNDO. (I have found my life.)
Woman . . . just to call you woman
Is the greatest compliment I can pay you.
Who are you, for I know
I've never seen you before, and yet
I know that once you felt something
For me, and I felt joy in seeing you?

ROSAURA. (It's important I hide who I am.)
I'm a sad lady, waiting on Estrella.

SEGISMUNDO. Don't say that; Estrella's just a star,
But you're the sun itself. She gets her light from you.
When I looked at the beautiful kingdom of flowers
I saw them governed by the beauty of the rose.
When I looked at the academy of stones
I saw them led by the brilliance of the diamond.
When I looked at the unquiet republic of stars
I found Venus to be the brightest of planets.
And when I looked at the harmony of planetary spheres
I saw the sun was the most beautiful of all.
So when I look at you, I just don't understand
How you, amidst flowers, amidst stars
Amidst spinning planets and precious stones
Could be serving someone of less beauty,
When you are the most beautiful
Diamond, sun, Venus, rose.

Enter CLOTALDO.

CLOTALDO (*aside*). (I want to help Segismundo see reason.
I brought him up. I feel responsible.
But what's happening now?)

ROSAURA. I'm moved by your compliments, but
    May silence make a speech for me.
    My reasoning feels clumsy, lord,
    And silence must be my best reply.

SEGISMUNDO. No wait, you mustn't go away.
    Why do you want to leave me in darkness?

ROSAURA. I ask permission to do so from your Highness.

SEGISMUNDO. If you're going to ask permission
    You should wait for my reply.
    For leaving before I give it, isn't
    Asking permission, but taking it.

ROSAURA. If you're not going to give permission
    Then I will take it.

SEGISMUNDO.   Then you'll make me change.
    Instead of being courteous, I'll be violent.
    Resistance is a poison kills my patience.

ROSAURA. This poison may well destroy
    All patience and self-restraint,
    Charged with fury, inhumanity
    And rage. But it wouldn't dare
    Force my consent. Nor could it.

SEGISMUNDO.   Perhaps I could.
    I'm getting curious to see. You're making me
    Lose all respect and fear of your beauty.
    Besides, I love doing what they tell me
    Can't be done. And only today
    I threw a man out the window
    Because he told me I couldn't do it.
    And right now I feel most inclined

To throw your honour out the window too.

CLOTALDO. (The situation's getting worse.
    What can I do, for heaven's sake,
    When yet again a mad desire
    Endangers my reputation.)

ROSAURA. They were obviously right to prophesy your
        cruelty
    And say that if you ruled this poor kingdom, it would
        suffer
    Betrayal, murder, treachery and civil war.
    But what else do you expect from a man
    A man so inhuman and so cruel, so vicious
    Violent and unrestrained, a man
    Human only in name, born and bred among wild
    animals?

SEGISMUNDO. I didn't want you to insult me like that.
    And I was trying to be courteous.
    I thought that might make you treat me better.
    But now you call me an animal
    And I didn't deserve that. But now,
    By Christ! I'll show you what it means.
    Get out. Leave us alone. Let no-one in.
    Bolt the door!

    Exit CLARIN.

ROSAURA.   Listen.

SEGISMUNDO. I'm an animal, remember? I'm not human
    any more.
    It's no use trying to make me change my mind.

CLOTALDO. (What a dreadful situation. Even if he kills me,

I must still prevent him.)
My Lord, wait, think . . .

SEGISMUNDO.   You feeble mad old man
You're provoking me again.
Do you really think so little of my cruelty and rage?
How did you get in here?

CLOTALDO. This voice called me. That's what brought
    me here.
I came to tell you not to be so proud
Not to be so wild. If you want to be king,
Rule peaceably. You may think you're the master here
But don't be cruel. It may turn out to be a dream.

SEGISMUNDO. When you talk of ending illusions,
When you talk of ending dreams,
You touch a kind of light in me
And it maddens me with rage!
But I know how I'll find out if this is true.
I'll find out by killing you.

As he pulls out his dagger, CLOTALDO *stops him, falling onto his knees.*

CLOTALDO. This is how I'll save myself.

SEGISMUNDO. Let go!

CLOTALDO. Until people come
Who can restrain
Your anger and rage
I won't let go!

SEGISMUNDO. Let go, feeble mad old man
Or I'll kill you.

They struggle.

ROSAURA. Quick, someone!
  The prince is killing Clotaldo!

Exit ROSAURA.

Enter ASTOLFO *just as* CLOTALDO *falls at his feet.
He stands between him and* SEGISMUNDO.

ASTOLFO. What are you doing, Prince?
  Staining your noble sword
  With an old man's cold blood?
  Put your sword away.

SEGISMUNDO. Only when I see it stained
  With this man's filthy blood.

ASTOLFO. He's fallen at my feet. He's asked for sanctuary.
  I'll make sure it does him good.

SEGISMUNDO. All it'll do is cause your death.
  And I'll get my revenge
  On the way that you insulted me.

ASTOLFO. This isn't treason. This is self-defence.

They draw their swords. Enter BASILIO *and* ESTRELLA.

CLOTALDO. Astolfo, don't attack him.

BASILIO. Are these drawn swords?

ESTRELLA (*aside*). (It's Astolfo. And I'm attacked by a grief
  That's filled with rage!)

BASILIO.   What happened?

ASTOLFO. Nothing, my lord, now you are here.

SEGISMUNDO. This isn't nothing, even if you are here.
　　I was trying to kill this old man . . .

BASILIO. Have you no respect for his age?

CLOTALDO. Your majesty, remember it's only me.
　　It really does not matter.

SEGISMUNDO. You expect me to respect old age?
　　Don't waste your time. Even you, old fool
　　You could find yourself one day
　　Begging for mercy at my feet.
　　You brought me up so cruelly
　　One day I'll get revenge.

　　Exit SEGISMUNDO.

BASILIO. Before that day comes
　　You'll go back to sleep
　　And when you wake up
　　You'll believe everything
　　You've seen and felt
　　Like all the world's good things
　　Were just a dream.

　　Exit BASILIO *and* CLOTALDO. ESTRELLA *and*
　　ASTOLFO *remain.*

ASTOLFO. My dear Estrella, how sad life is.
　　When a horoscope predicts
　　Misfortunes, it's generally correct:
　　Any evil it predicts is certain:
　　Any good it predicts is dubious.
　　This can be absolutely proven
　　In the case of Segismundo and myself,
　　For the opposite was predicted for each.

For him was foretold unpleasantness, misfortune
Deaths. And we can see for ourselves
How all of it is coming true.
The prognosis was bad, its accuracy excellent.
As for myself, I was predicted
Good fortune, happiness, pleasure, glory.
But one glance from your extraordinary eyes
Whose brilliance dims the sun and makes even the sky
A pale reflection of its former glory
Make me understand, dear lady, all too well,
The prognosis was excellent, but its accuracy dubious.

ESTRELLA. I'm absolutely sure these flatteries
Are utterly and totally sincere
But meant for someone else.
Perhaps for the lady whose portrait
You carried round your neck
When you first came to see me.
And so, obviously, these gorgeous compliments
Deserve to be heard by her.
You should go and make sure she returns them
For in love's counting house, Astolfo,
I'm afraid they count as forgeries
Bills of love made out in someone else's name

Enter ROSAURA, *where the other characters cannot see her.*

ROSAURA *(aside).* (My misfortunes have reached the
   absolute limit!
And thank god for that, for any lover who sees this happen
Has seen the worst and has nothing more to fear.)

ASTOLFO. In the presence of a diamond,
A magnet loses its strength.

In the presence of an emerald
A poison loses its venom
And, confronted with the sun,
A star loses its splendour.
And so, my lady, that portrait
When it came and saw you, lost
All strength, power and loveliness
Because your beauty conquered it.

ESTRELLA. If I had really conquered it, Astolfo,
It would run away when it saw me
For the vanquished always run
From the place where they are defeated.

ASTOLFO. Then I will ensure it leaves this place
And then, like a defeated slave,
Kneels and kisses your delightful feet.
(Beautiful Rosaura, forgive me
For demeaning you. But for men and women
Who are separated, this is faithfulness.)

Exit ASTOLFO.

ROSAURA (*aside*). (I was so worried about being seen
I never heard a thing!)

ESTRELLA. Astrea.

ROSAURA.   My lady.

ESTRELLA. I'm so pleased it is you. For you are the
only one
To whom I dare entrust this secret.

ROSAURA. My lady, you honour me. I am ready to
obey you.

ESTRELLA. In the little time I have known you
    You have won the key to my soul.
    For this reason, and because you are,
    The person that you are, I now entrust to you
    A secret that so often I have feared to disclose
    Even to myself.

ROSAURA.   Tell me your wish.

ESTRELLA.   Well . . .
    To be brief . . . my cousin Astolfo,
    To say he's my cousin is more than enough . . .
    There are things one should express
    Only in thought . . . he is to marry me.
    Or at least he will if the world allows
    One piece of good fortune to remove
    So many other sources of grief.
    It hurt me to see hanging round his neck
    The portrait of another lady.
    I asked him for it courteously;
    He is polite and wishes well.
    He went to fetch it and will bring it here
    It will embarrass me if he comes here
    And gives it to me face to face.
    Please tell him to give it you, and . . .
    I'll say no more. You are beautiful
    And you are also discreet.
    You know what love is very well.

    Exit ESTRELLA.

ROSAURA. And I wish I didn't know a thing about it!
    God help me! Who could ever be clever enough
    To know what advice to give herself

In such an impossible situation!
Can there be anyone in the whole world
Attacked by so much misfortune
Besieged by so much pain?
What will I do in such confusion
Where it seems impossible to find
Any reason to comfort me
Or any comfort to console me?
After the first misfortune
There is no happening or event
That isn't another source of grief!
One after another they keep coming.
One gives birth to the next
Like the phoenix, each new misfortune
Arises from the ashes of the one before!
And they never get cold in their graves.
Someone said once that misfortunes
Are cowards because you never see any
On their own. I say they're brave.
They always keep advancing
And never turn their back.
Clotaldo tells me to keep quiet,
My shame tells me to wait.
Estrella tells me to be a go-between,
Love tells me to sort it out.
And I know jealousy's
Something it's impossible to conceal.
So what can I do to straighten out
Such a tangled knotted mess!
But what's the use of trying to prepare
Or thinking what I ought to do or say.
It's obvious that when the moment comes

Grief will do what it must,
For there's no-one anywhere in the world
That can ever control their anguish?
Well, since my soul does not dare decide
What must be done, let my grief go on
As far as it dares or can, and let my pain
Travel to its far extreme and so leave me free
Free from doubts and wondering what to do.
But till then – God help me. Heaven give me strength!

Enter ASTOLFO.

ASTOLFO. This is the portrait, my lady . . .

ROSAURA. Why does your highness hesitate?
Why does your highness stand amazed?

ASTOLFO. Amazed to see you, Rosaura, and to hear
you speak.

ROSAURA. Why are you calling me Rosaura?
Your Highness is mistaken, and takes me
For some other lady. For I am Astrea,
And in my humble state do not deserve
The great happiness of seeing you so perturbed.

ASTOLFO. Rosaura, that's enough deception.
The soul never lies
And although I see you as Astrea
I love you as Rosaura.

ROSAURA. All I can tell you is that Estrella
– But perhaps I should call her Aphrodite! –
Asked me to await you here
And to tell you on her behalf
To hand over that portrait

Of the lady who once passed through your life.
That is what Estrella wants
And even in the smallest things
She must always be obeyed
Even when they cause me grief.

ASTOLFO. However hard you try, Rosaura,
How badly you pretend! Tell your eyes
To harmonise their music with your voice;
For it's an instrument that's out of tune,
Full of discord and dissonance,
Trying in vain to conceal the gulf
Between the falsehood that it speaks
And the deep truth it feels.

ROSAURA. All I can say to you is
That I'm waiting for the portrait.

ASTOLFO. Well if you wish to continue this deception
I'll continue it in my reply.
Astrea, you will tell the princess
That I so greatly esteem her that
When she asked me for a portrait
It seemed to me so small a thing
To send it on its own, and so,
Because I esteem and value her,
I'm sending the original.

ROSAURA. When there's something that a man intends
And he's decisive, proud and brave
He has to find what he's resolved to
Or he turns back covered in shame.
I came for a portrait, and it's true
I do possess an original worth far more.

I'll still return a failure if I return alone
And so, your highness, give me the miniature
For I refuse to leave without it.

ASTOLFO. But how do you propose to take it
If I don't intend to give it?

ROSAURA. Like this.

She tries to take it from him.

You betrayed me! Let it go!

ASTOLFO. It's no use struggling.

ROSAURA. I swear to God I'll never see it
In that woman's hands! I'd rather die!

ASTOLFO.   You're frightening.

ROSAURA. You're disgusting!

ASTOLFO. Rosaura my dear, that's quite enough.

ROSAURA. I'm not yours. You liar!

Enter ESTRELLA.

ESTRELLA. Astrea, Astolfo, what is this?

ASTOLFO. (Oh God, here comes Estrella!)

ROSAURA. (God of love be kind. Give me cunning.)
If you want to know what's happening, my lady,
I will tell you.

ASTOLFO.   (Now she's done for!)

ROSAURA. You asked me to wait here
For Astolfo, and ask him for a miniature.
I was alone for a moment, and since in the mind

One thing leads to another so easily,
As you spoke of miniatures, I remembered
I had one of my own in this sleeve.
I've never met my father, and I had it made for him.
I wanted to see it for when one's alone.
It's always trivial things that pass the time.
It fell from my hand onto the floor.
Astolfo, coming to give you the other miniature,
Picked it up, and is so unwilling to give you
The thing you ask of him, that instead of giving
One picture, he wished to take another.
And when I asked him, and tried to persuade him
To return it me, he refused point blank.
I became angry and impatient
And tried to take it.
That's my portrait he holds in his hand;
As to whether if it's a likeness,
Take it and see for yourself.

ESTRELLA. Astolfo, give me that picture!

She takes it from him.

ASTOLFO. My lady!

ESTRELLA.   It's flattering.

ROSAURA.   Is it not mine?

ESTRELLA. What doubt could there possibly be?

ROSAURA. Well, since this picture's mine,
     Tell him to give you the other one.

ESTRELLA. Take your picture and be gone.

ROSAURA. (I've got my picture back;
    I don't care what happens now.)

    Exit ROSAURA.

ESTRELLA. Now you give me the picture
    That I asked from you. For although
    I no longer have any plans
    To see you or speak to you again,
    I still definitely do not want
    To see it in your power even if
    Simply because I embarrassed myself
    In asking for it.

ASTOLFO.   Lady, please take note.

ESTRELLA. There's nothing I have to note.
    You have to give me the picture.

ASTOLFO. (How can I get out of this?)
    Beautiful Estrella, I would dearly love
    To serve you and obey you, I still cannot
    Give you the portrait, because . . .

ESTRELLA.   How gross!
    I don't want you to give it to me now
    Because I don't ever want you to remind me
    That I ever asked you for it.

    Exit ESTRELLA.

ASTOLFO. No stop, listen, wait!
    When, where and how, Rosaura,
    Have you managed to come here
    To destroy us both!

    Exit ASTOLFO.

SEGISMUNDO *is discovered as at the beginning, dressed in skins, bound with chains, asleep on the ground. Enter* CLOTALDO, CLARIN *and* TWO SERVANTS.

CLOTALDO. This is where
You leave him
And pride ends
Where it began.

SERVANT 1. I've just tied him to the chain
Like he was before.

CLARIN. Segismundo, don't wake up.
Don't find yourself
With your good fortune turned to bad.
Don't see how all your glory was a sham,
A shadow of life,
A flame of death.

CLOTALDO. Anyone who can speak like that
Needs to have a space prepared
Where he has lots of room to argue in.
This is the one you have to seize
And lock up in that cell.

CLARIN. Why me?

CLOTALDO.   Because it's important to imprison
A Clarín who knows so many secrets
In case he starts to sing.

CLARIN. No wait a minute. Did I try to kill my father?
Did I throw anyone out the window
To see if they might fly?
Am I a King's son?
Am I dreaming? Am I awake?
Why lock me up?

CLOTALDO. You're Clarín.

CLARIN. From the Latin. Clarion.
    All right I'll be a cornet, and shut up,
    Or the man with the little triangle that sits at the back
    And never gets to play a note.

They carry him off.

Enter KING BASILIO, *muffled in a cloak.*

BASILIO. Clotaldo?

CLOTALDO. Your majesty! You have come here?

BASILIO. I felt a foolish curiosity to see
    What will happen to Segismundo
    And I felt a foolish grief.

CLOTALDO. Look at him now returned
    To his old state of misery.

BASILIO. My sad unfortunate prince,
    Born at the wrong time!
    Go and wake him now
    For the drug you gave him
    Must surely have lost its strength.

CLOTALDO. My lord, he is restless
    He's speaking in his sleep.

BASILIO. What will he be dreaming of?
    Let's listen.

SEGISMUNDO (*in his dreams*). A good king should
        punish injustice.
    It's my duty to kill Clotaldo.
    I must make my father my slave.

CLOTALDO. He threatens me with death.

BASILIO. He threatens me with servitude.

CLOTALDO. He wants to kill me.

BASILIO. He wants me to be his slave.

SEGISMUNDO. Returning to stage by popular demand,
   Featuring in the great theatre of the world
   The courageous prince Segismundo
   Who takes revenge on his wicked father!

He wakes up.

Where am I? Oh no . . . no!

BASILIO. He must not see me.
   You know what you must do.
   I'll be listening from here.

The KING *withdraws.*

SEGISMUNDO. Is this me?
   Is this really me?
   Back in chains again.
   Back in my prison.
   Back in my grave.
   Yes. God help me.
   Dear God, the things I've dreamed!

CLOTALDO (*aside*). (And now I'm supposed to complete
   the deception.)
   So it's time to wake up, is it?

SEGISMUNDO. Yes, it's time to wake up.

CLOTALDO. Are you going to sleep the whole day?
   You mean you've been sleeping since the time
   We spoke of that proud eagle's flight?

SEGISMUNDO.   Yes
    Clotaldo, and I think I'm still asleep.
    And I can't be that far wrong
    For if everything was a dream
    Everything I saw and touched for sure
    Then anything could be a dream,
    Everything I see and touch just now.
    And it seems very possible now
    Now I am so utterly defeated
    That even though I'm sleeping I can still see
    That even though I'm waking I can still dream.

CLOTALDO. Tell me what you dreamed.

SEGISMUNDO. Supposing that it was a dream
    I won't tell you what I dreamt, Clotaldo.
    I'll tell you what I saw.
    I woke up and found myself –
    And this was a lie, Clotaldo,
    A cruel and flattering lie! Because
    I was in a bed so brightly coloured
    It could have been a bed of flowers
    Woven by the goddess of spring.
    A thousand nobles bowed down to me,
    Called me their prince, and served me
    With perfumes, jewels, and fine clothes.
    My senses were in turmoil;
    You turned them into joy
    By telling me my good fortune.
    For even though this is how I am
    There I was a Prince of Poland.

CLOTALDO. And did you reward me for this good news?

SEGISMUNDO. No. Because you were a traitor
  I summoned up all my bold courage
  And I killed you twice.

CLOTALDO. You hated me so much?

SEGISMUNDO. I was lord of all
  And took my revenge on everyone.
  I only loved one woman
  And I think that love was true
  Because everything else ended.
  But that love goes on and on.

  Exit the KING.

CLOTALDO. (The king was moved by what he heard,
      and left.)
  It's because we spoke about
  That eagle, you dreamt of empires;
  But even dreaming it's a good idea to treat me well
  Because I've done my best to bring you up
  And Segismundo, even when you're dreaming.
  The good you do is never lost.

  Exit.

SEGISMUNDO. What if he's right? What if we suppressed
  This ferocity, this ambition and this rage
  Just in case it is a dream.
  Yes, let's do that, for this life's so strange
  Living it is just a dream.
  That's what experience teaches me:
  That everyone who lives is only dreaming
  Who they are till they awake.
  The king dreams he is a king, and lives

Governing under this deception,
Making laws and ruling;
And the applause, which he receives,
He gets it as a loan, and it's written in the wind
And death turns it all to ashes.
And that's such a terrible thing!
Is there anyone who'd want to rule
Knowing that they must wake up
Wake up in the sleep of death!
The rich man dreams of his riches
Which just offer him more cares.
The poor man dreams he suffers
His misery and poverty.
The one who tries to get on in life is dreaming
The one who ambitiously and obsessively strives
The one who hurts, insults and offends
And in this world, in the end,
Everyone dreams they are who they are
Although no-one understands this.
I dream that I am here
Bound down by these heavy chains
And I dreamed that once I lived differently
And was happy.
What is life? A frenzy.
Life's an illusion.
Life's a shadow, a fiction,
And the greatest good is worth nothing at all,
For the whole of life is just a dream
And dreams . . . dreams are only dreams.

End of Act Two.

ACT THREE

Enter CLARIN, *on his own, in the dark.*

CLARIN. Here I am. Locked up in a magic tower
   Imprisoned for what I know.
   So what about what I don't know?
   What'll they do to me for that?
   They'll kill me. They're killing me already.
   For someone as hungry as me
   Is slowly but surely dying.
   I feel sorry for myself.
   I know you're all going to think
   'Well I'm not at all surprised'
   And you're right. It's all terribly predictable.
   It's terrible to have a name like Clarin
   And be silent. Clarin. You know. From the Latin.
   And I'm all alone with no-one to talk to
   But spiders and rats. And their conversation
   Leaves a lot to be desired.
   And my poor head's full of dreams.
   I keep dreaming of trumpets.
   And people whipping themselves
   In processions, and other people
   Watching them and fainting.
   And some go up and some go down
   And I just stay in the same place

Fainting for lack of food.
I'm on a starvation diet
And it's worse than the diet of Worms.
If I were a philosopher,
I'd be in the anorexic school of thought.
And I don't get any holidays or feast days
Or anydays but hungry days.
I'm all dazed. And I deserve it:
Because I had a bit of knowledge and I didn't share it.
Servants are meant to talk in plays
And I haven't said a word.

There's a sound of drums within, and shouting.

SOLDIER 2. Here he is. This is the tower.
Kick in the door!
Come on in.

CLARIN. Christ they must be looking for me.
They've just said here I am.
What do they want me for?
Are these people looking for me?

Enter as many SOLDIERS *as possible.*

SOLDIER 1. Come on!

SOLDIER 2. Here he is!

CLARIN. No he isn't.

ALL. Your majesty!

CLARIN. Are they drunk?

SOLDIER 2. You are our Prince
For we don't want and we won't accept

Anyone except our own real prince
And we don't want any foreigner.

ALL. Long live our great prince!

CLARIN. I think they really mean it!
Maybe in this kingdom it's the custom
Maybe they take someone every day, make him prince
And then lock him up again?
They did it yesterday. I saw them.
So this is them doing it today.
I'd better play the part.

SOLDIERS. Allow us to kiss your feet.

CLARIN. No I can't do that, I haven't washed them.
Anyway they're my feet and I like them.
Don't want anyone fooling around with them
Footling around with them.
It would be footless. Fruitless.
But thank you anyway.

SOLDIER 2. We all went to your father and we told him
You're the only prince we'll recognise
And not that foreigner from Moscow.

CLARIN. Are you telling me you were rude to my dad?
You're a lot of rotten shits.

SOLDIER 1. We only did it out of loyalty.

CLARIN. Oh well if it was loyalty, I forgive you

SOLDIER 2. Come out and restore your Empire!
Long live Segismundo!

ALL. Long live Segismundo!

CLARIN. Are they calling me Segismundo? Oh well.
    Obviously they call all their fake princes
    Segismundo.

    Enter SEGISMUNDO.

SEGISMUNDO. Who calls for me?

CLARIN. That's the end of me as prince.
    Now I'm the artist formerly known as
    Blank.

SOLDIER 2. So who is Segismundo?

SEGISMUNDO. Me

SOLDIER 2. So what were you doing, you stupid, rash fool
    Calling yourself Segismundo?

CLARIN. How dare you. I never did. Call myself
        Segismundo . . .
    You were the ones who were Segismundo-ing me.
    So you're the ones who's stupid and rash.

SOLDIER 1. Great prince Segismundo
    Your father, king Basilio, was afraid
    Of some prophecy which said
    He would find himself helpless at your feet.
    He wants to take away from you your power
    And your right to rule
    And give it all to Astolfo, Duke of Moscow.
    That's what he told his court, and the people got to
        know of this
    And once we knew we have a real king
    We don't want to be ruled by a foreigner.

And so we've come to find you
Where they're keeping you prisoner.
We bring you weapons and an army
So you can lead a revolution
To depose a tyrant and restore yourself
As rightful ruler. Come then:
For out in this wasteland a huge army
Is waiting to acclaim you.
Freedom awaits you Prince:
Hear its shouts.

VOICES (*within*). long live Segismundo!

SEGISMUNDO. Yet again am I supposed to dream
Another vision of greatness and power
Which will be destroyed by time?
Yet again am I supposed to see
Dimly amidst mists and shadows
Another vision of pompous majesty?
Yet again am I supposed to feel
The pain of disillusionment and loss
That all human power is subject to
And must humbly live and alertly watch for?
I won't do it. I won't. I won't!
Go away you figments! You illusions
Deceiving my dead senses
With the appearance of bodies and voices
When you have no body and you have no voice!
I don't want false power.
I don't want false majesty!
You fantastical illusions
That will disappear at the first breath of dawn,
You're like the blossom on the almond tree

Who flowers so foolishly soon
And then withers, fades, and loses
From its rosy buds all beauty,
All delight, all ornament,
Blown away by the first breath of winter wind.
You see I know you now
I know it's just the same with you
And with anyone who's dreaming.
Now there's no way I can be deceived
My eyes are opened, I have no illusions
And I know life is just a dream.

SOLDIER 2. You think we're fooling you
And it just isn't true. Turn your eyes
And look up at that proud mountain.
You'll see there's a crowd of people there
Waiting to do whatever you tell them.

SEGISMUNDO. I saw all that before, and it looked
As clear and as distinct
As everything that I see now
And it was all a dream.

SOLDIER 1. When great things happen, lord, they
always come with premonitions
And that's what that was, if you dreamed it first.

SEGISMUNDO. You're right; it was a premonition
(And so just in case it is true
And since life is a dream,
Let's dream, my soul,
Let's dream again but this time with attention
And bearing in mind that at some fine time
We're going to wake up from this pleasure.

Because if we know that
It'll all come as less of a shock.
And it's always best to be one step ahead
Of pain. So, taking this precaution,
And knowing that all power is on loan
And will have to be given back to its owner
Let's dare to do everything.
Friends, I appreciate your loyalty.
You'll find in me
Someone clever enough and brave enough
To free you from foreign rule.
Call to arms! Prepare to march!
My courage will never be defeated!
I will fight my own father and defeat him!
I will make the prophecy come true!
And he will be lying helpless at my feet!
(But if before this I wake up
wouldn't it be better not to say it
since I'm not going to do it?)

ALL. Long live Segismundo!
   Long live freedom!

   Enter CLOTALDO.

CLOTALDO. What is this?

SEGISMUNDO. Clotaldo!

CLOTALDO. My lord!
   (I expect I'll be the first target of his cruelty.)

CLARIN. (I bet he throws him off the mountain.)

   Exit.

CLOTALDO. I kneel before you. I know I shall die.

SEGISMUNDO. Father, get up, don't stay on your knees.
   I want you to guide me
   In what I have to do.
   I know I owe my upbringing
   To your love and loyalty.
   Embrace me.

CLOTALDO. What are you saying?

SEGISMUNDO. I am dreaming and I want to do good.
   For the good you do is never lost,
   Not even in dreams.

CLOTALDO. Well, my lord, if doing good
   Is what you now intend, then obviously
   It won't offend you if I try to do the same.
   You are about to make war on your father;
   I can't advise you in a war against my king
   Or be of any use to you.
   Here I am at your feet: kill me.

SEGISMUNDO. You peasant, you wretch, you traitor,
   (God I need to control myself!
   I'm not even sure if I'm awake!
   It's like putting a brake on all my rage
   This thought that I'm going to wake up
   And find myself without this power!)

SOLDIER 2. All this loyalty's a waste of time.
   What you're really doing is ignoring the common good.
   We're the ones that are loyal because we're making sure
   That it's our real prince who governs us.

CLOTALDO. That would be fine once the king was dead
   But the king is still alive and must be obeyed

As our only ruler; and nothing can ever justify
His vassals taking arms against him.

SOLDIER 2. Well we'll soon see Clotaldo
How much this loyalty is worth.

CLOTALDO. The main thing is to obey orders

SEGISMUNDO. That's enough!

CLOTALDO. My lord.

SEGISMUNDO.
Clotaldo, I envy you your bravery
And I'm grateful for it.
Go and serve the king.
We'll meet on the battlefield.
But let's not argue
Whether it's a good thing or a bad.
We all have our sense of honour.

CLOTALDO. I won't forget my gratitude.

Exit.

SEGISMUNDO. You, beat the drum for war
And march in good order.
Head for the king's palace!

ALL. Long live our great prince!

SEGISMUNDO. Fortune, we're going to be king.
Don't wake me up, if I'm dreaming;
If it's real, then don't send me back to sleep.
But whether it's real or whether it's a dream
Doing good is all that matters
If it's real, then just because;

If it's a dream, to win friends
For when we wake up again.

They exit. Drums beat.

Enter BASILIO *and* ASTOLFO.

BASILIO. When a horse goes mad and starts to run
Is there anyone strong enough to halt it?
Can anyone stop a raging river on a slope
Tumbling wildly down jagged rocks to the sea?
Can anyone stop a torn off mountain crag
Crashing uncontrollably to the valley below?
All these things would be easier to control
Than the fierce energy of the common people.
All we see and hear attests this truth.
The shouts of opposing factions echo across the valleys.
Some call out 'Segismundo' some 'Astolfo'.
The throne room has become a side show
A dismal theatre, an empty auditorium
Where fortune mounts tragedies no-one wants to see.

ASTOLFO. All rejoicing has to be postponed,
All applause brought to a sudden halt
Every good fortune promised by your fortunate hand,
For if Poland – which I hope to rule –
Now resists the obedience it owes me
It is simply so I can earn the right to it.
Bring me a horse, and, full of pride,
I'll boast like thunder and descend
Like a bolt of lightning.

Exit ASTOLFO.

BASILIO. Nothing can be done against the infallibly true.
    There is great danger in tampering with the foreseen.
    If something has to happen, nothing can prevent it,
    And the more you try to stop it
    The more you make it actually occur.
    How harsh a law. How terrifying a fact. How cruel
        a universe.
    Anyone who thinks they are avoiding a risk
    Is in fact walking right into it. Trying to save myself,
    I have dug my own grave.
    I tried to overcome a danger
    And I have brought it about.
    I tried to save my country
    And I have destroyed it.

Enter ESTRELLA.

ESTRELLA. Great king, you have to prevent this riot
    Breaking out among rival mobs, tearing
    Each other apart in the city streets.
    Otherwise your kingdom will drown in blood
    An ocean of bloodshed will overwhelm it.
    For now in the streets walks nothing but misfortune.
    Now in the streets screams nothing but tragedy.
    So great is the ruin of your empire
    So great the rage and thirst for blood
    All eyes are filled with terror
    All ears with the wounded's screams.
    The sun is darkened, the wind breathes fear,
    Each stone marks a grave
    Each flower a funeral wreath
    Each building a cemetery
    And each soldier a living skeleton.

Enter CLOTALDO.

CLOTALDO. Thank god I'm alive to fall at your feet!

BASILIO. Clotaldo! What news of Segismundo?

CLOTALDO. The people, like a blinded monster
A boulder rolling down a mountain,
Have reached the tower and set him free.
For the second time, he finds himself honoured
And treated like a king, and has sworn
To dethrone you, fiercely declaring
That he will make heaven's prophecies come true.

BASILIO. Then bring me a horse, and my weary old age
Will ride out to subdue a rebellious son.
And when it comes to defending my throne,
Perhaps where science failed, violence will prevail.

ESTRELLA. I have fought a fierce battle against jealousy
So a battlefield for me holds no terrors.
I'll ride after you and swing my sword
Striking men dead with each fierce blow.

Exit BASILIO *and* ESTRELLA.

ROSAURA. All is war. And I know your courage
Screams within you to urge you join it, but
Please hear me. I came here poor, lonely and humiliated.
Out of nobility you sheltered and took pity on me.
I was obliged to you, obliged to follow
Your advice, dress as a woman, live
In the palace, conceal my true self
And serve Estrella, my beautiful enemy.
Astolfo saw me, knows who I am
And acts with such utter disregard of me

He has made an assignation with Estrella
For tonight in the palace garden.
I have the key. You can enter it.
With pride, courage and determination
You can end my shame.
I know you have already decided
To avenge me by killing him.
Take your chance. I want his death.
Kill the man who has betrayed me.

CLOTALDO. It's true that I did find myself inclined
        Rosaura, from the moment I first saw you,
        Inclined towards doing all I could to help you
        And your weeping was the witness.
        I intended to help you take revenge.
        The first step I took was to have you change your clothes
        So that if Astolfo saw you, he would see you
        Dressed as a woman, and so would not judge
        Your absurd rashness as a sign of promiscuity.
        At that time I was trying to find the means
        To recover your lost honour, and did even consider
        – And judge from this how far my concern was taking
            me –
        Killing Astolfo. What an absurd notion!
        Even though, given he is not my King
        I could contemplate his murder without astonishment
        Or dismay. I was about to kill him when Segismundo
        Tried to kill me. Astolfo came, showed courage,
        Ignored his own safety, and saved my life.
        So how am I supposed to repay
        This man who gave me life
        By giving him death in return?

I don't know what to do. I want
To give you an honourable life
And that pulls me one way;
But I am obliged to him for the fact
That I'm still living at all.
Torn between giving and receiving,
I am an agent, and a patient too:
Caught in the slipstream, uncertain, undecided,
A person who acts; a soul who suffers.

ROSAURA. You know perfectly well that it's nobler
To give than it is to receive. Giving
Puts you in a position of strength:
Receiving puts you at a disadvantage.
So think of the difference between him and me.
I have enabled you to give, and strengthened you
But he has forced you to receive, and weakened you.
So you are more beholden to me; not him,
And in this dangerous time you must
Come over to me. For I take precedence,
Just as giving is nobler than receiving.

CLOTALDO. I agree the act of giving is noble. But
It calls for gratitude from the receiver.
A reputation for generosity I already possess;
Allow me now to gain what I lack:
A reputation for gratitude.

ROSAURA. You gave me life; but you told me yourself
That life without self-respect, life
Lived under the weight of insult,
Is not life at all. It's a kind of death.
You say you want to be generous.

So be generous. Give me life.
The only true life: life free from dishonour.
Be generous first. You can be grateful afterwards.

CLOTALDO. Rosaura, I'm sure you're right.
Generosity matters more.
So I'll give you all my property
So you can enter a convent and there live in peace.
This resolves the situation, for it
Gives you refuge from your shame.
And with the whole kingdom
In a state of civil war, I refuse
To kill Astolfo, my prince, and so add
To my country's deep misfortunes.
You see this solves everything:
I can be loyal to my country,
Show generosity to you and
Gratitude to Astolfo.
So it's important you agree,
For I could hardly do more,
For heavens sake! – if I was your father.

ROSAURA. If you were my father
I might put up with this.
But since you're not, I won't.

CLOTALDO. So what do you intend to do?

ROSAURA.   Kill Astolfo.

CLOTALDO. Can a girl who's never known her father
Have the courage to do such a thing?

ROSAURA.   Yes.

CLOTALDO. What drives you on?

ROSAURA.   My self-respect.

CLOTALDO. Remember you have to see Astolfo –

ROSAURA. As the man who's insulted and betrayed me.

CLOTALDO. – As your king and husband to Estrella.

ROSAURA. That will never be. I swear to God.

CLOTALDO. This is madness.

ROSAURA.   I know.

CLOTALDO.   Then overcome it.

ROSAURA. I cannot.

CLOTALDO.   Then you will lose . . .

ROSAURA.   Yes.

CLOTALDO. Life and honour.

ROSAURA.   I know.

CLOTALDO. What are you hoping to achieve?

ROSAURA. My death.

CLOTALDO.   This is worse than desperate.

ROSAURA. It is honour.

CLOTALDO.   It's madness.

ROSAURA.   Bravery.

CLOTALDO. It's sheer lunacy.

ROSAURA.   It's anger, it's rage.

CLOTALDO. You're possessed by a hatred
    You won't even try to control?

ROSAURA. No.

CLOTALDO.   Who will help you?

ROSAURA.   I'll help myself.

CLOTALDO. Is there no alternative?

ROSAURA.   No.

CLOTALDO. There has to be. Rosaura please.
    There has to be another way.

ROSAURA. Another way to destroy myself!

    Exit ROSAURA.

CLOTALDO.   Daughter!
    Well, if you insist on being destroyed,
    Let's destroy ourselves together!

    Exit CLOTALDO.

    They beat the drum, and enter SEGISMUNDO, *dressed in skins,*
    with CLARIN *and* MARCHING SOLDIERS.

SEGISMUNDO. I wish the Roman Emperors could see
    me now
    Dressed like an animal, leading an army
    Ready for anything! I could defeat the sky!
    No. Wait, don't get too ambitious. Don't aim so high
    Don't make it all disappear, or this dream of greatness
    Will hurt me when I wake up and find it gone.
    The less I have to lose, the less I suffer when it
    disappears.

CLARIN. There's a man with his eyes wide open
    But still living in the dark. It's madness.
    He can see everything, but can't make sense of it.

And I'm as bad. Here's me, seeing him,
And not making sense of him at all.

A clarion call within. Drums.

SEGISMUNDO. What's that?

CLARIN.   A swift horse. And, I'm sorry,
But I have to describe it. It's my cue.
It's a horse on which the learned can see a map.
For its body is the earth,
The fire its soul all locked up in its chest
The sea is the foam that's all spewed up at its mouth
And the air's its panting breath.
Now this is confusing and extremely chaotic
For in its soul, foam, body and breath
It's a monster of fire, water, wind and earth,
A piebald monster, dappled all over, bridled and spurred
By the person who's riding her
And who doesn't just gallop but flies
Into your presence and is a woman

SEGISMUNDO. Whose beauty blinds me.

CLARIN. For goodness sake it's Rosaura!

Exit CLARIN.

SEGISMUNDO. Fate has brought her back to me.
Everything I dreamed of is coming true.

Enter ROSAURA *wearing a gorgeous dress, a sword and a
dagger.*

ROSAURA. Segismundo, noble prince, rising
Like the sun after years of darkness
Rising, crowned and majestic,

In the arms of dawn,
Glittering like a jewel,
On flowers, roses, mountain tops,
The flecks of foam on the crests of the waves:
I know you will help me because you are noble
And I am a woman in need of assistance.
This is the third time you have seen and admired me
Yet the third time you do not know me
For each time we meet I have appeared
In a different shape, dress and form.
The first time you saw me you were held in chains.
You saw me in your prison and you thought me a man
And you helped me through a time of dark misfortune.
The second time you saw me you were treated as a king.
I was dressed as a woman, you were admiring of my
    beauty
In your illusory dream of power and majesty.
Today is the third time and I'm a kind of monster
Carrying man's weapons, but wearing women's clothes
And so that you may now take pity
And be spurred on the better to help me
I must tell you my sad story.
They say beauty and misfortune go hand in hand.
My mother was unfortunate enough
To be most beautiful. She was a noble Muscovite;
A man fell in love with her,
A man I cannot name because I do not know it.
I know he had courage, because I have courage too.
And in my grief at the circumstance of my birth
I would imagine him to be a kind of god,
Those you find in the ancient stories
And whose victims weep, like Danae, like Leda,

Because gods, like men, forget the women
Who once gave them pleasure.
I was afraid I was lengthening my story
By quoting all these ancient, frivolous tales.
But now I've discover that I've told it all.
My mother was as beautiful as any
And as unhappy as them all.
It was a promise of marriage,
That same old stupid story,
Which took such a hold on her mind.
She still expects it to be fulfilled.
The man was like Aeneas in the siege of Troy,
So great a betrayer of faith
That he even left his sword behind.
I'll sheathe it here and when the story ends
The time will come to show it naked to the world.
The promise of marriage is like a knot
That's been badly tied, it does not bind,
It gives no shelter nor protection,
But I was born from it. Born so like my mother
If not in beauty, then at least
In how I lived and suffered
And what I allowed happen to me.
The man who wrecked my reputation
And destroyed my self-respect
Is . . . Astolfo. My face flares up,
And the simple act of naming him
Fills my heart with anger and with rage
Which is exactly what you would expect
When you name a vicious enemy.
Astolfo was the wretched man
Who forgot all of our love's glories

Just like you'd forget the name
Of some chance acquaintance,
Betrayed me, left for Poland
Aiming for another conquest,
This time with the beautiful Estrella.
She was the guide for my descent into darkness.
If it really was a star
That brought us together as lovers.
How ironic that now Estrella
Should be the unlucky star to divide us.
He lied to me. He insulted me.
He left me drowning in madness and grief.
Inside me boiled the confusion of Babylon
And burned the pitiless fires of hell.
I never spoke of this. Some griefs
Are best spoken of in silence.
Until one day alone with my mother,
I broke down their prison door
And they all burst out at once
Tripping over each other in their haste.
I will not shame myself repeating them;
But I could freely speak to her
Because I knew she had suffered similar pain.
Sometimes a bad example is of some use.
She took pity on me in my tears,
Consoled me with her own, forgave me.
Forgiveness is easy when you have also sinned.
Learning a lesson from her own life story
– for she had left it all to be sorted out by time,
And had been left alone with her misfortunes –
She thought it best that I follow Astolfo
And having found him, force him to repay his debt.

To try to lessen the damage to my battered reputation.
She thought it best I go dressed as a man.
She took down an ancient sword,
The one that I am now wearing
– And it is time I fulfilled my promise
And unsheathed its naked blade –
And there she told me 'Go to Poland
Rosaura, dressed as a man,
And there make sure the noblest men
See you with this sword. For it could be
That in one you will find a friend
To take pity on your griefs
And remedy your misfortunes'.
And so I came to Poland.
I won't describe how a maddened horse
Led me to your prison where you languished
In chains and darkness, and there first saw me.
I won't describe how Clotaldo
Became so passionately involved in my misfortune
How the king spares my life for him;
How, once I'd told him who I am,
Clotaldo persuades me to put on women's clothes
And serve Estrella, where I'm clever enough
To disturb Astolfo's wooing.
I won't describe how you saw me there,
Admiring me, confused because you'd seen me
Wearing clothes of two different forms.
But now I'll tell you that Clotaldo
Became convinced that it matters
That Astolfo and the beautiful Estrella marry
And become rulers of Poland together.
And so he advised me to drop my claim,

And live in a convent and there languish
Sad and inconsolable. But now,
Brave Segismundo, now that fate
Has set you free from your dark prison
That place where you have been
Like a wild animal in your fierce anger
And like an unbroken rock of patient suffering
Now you have the chance to take revenge.
And seeing this, I have decided to join you,
Wearing both the gorgeous dress of Aphrodite
And the god of war's impenetrable steel.
Both adorn me as we meet for this third time.
And I've come both to oblige you and assist you
Coming as a woman to persuade you
To help me regain my honour
And coming as a man to assist you
To help you regain your throne.
As a woman I come to inspire your pity
When I beg you at your feet
As a man I come to serve you with courage
When your army enters the fight
As a woman I come so you can rescue me
In my insult and my dishonour
And as a man I have come to fight for you
With my sword and my fierce presence.
And so it seems to me that today
If I fall in love with you as a woman
As a man I will die for you
Fiercely defending my honour.
It matters to us both, brave leader,
That this arranged wedding does not take place.
It matters to me so that the man

Who calls himself my husband does not marry;
It matters to you because you need to prevent
The union of their powers which may put in doubt
Our own inevitable victory.
As a woman, I come to persuade you
To take up arms in defence of my honour;
As a man I come to encourage you
To recover your lost sceptre.
As a woman, I come to beg for your pity
When I fall helpless at your feet.
As a man I come to aid you
With my sword and my fierce courage.
If you love me as a woman
As a man I'll fight to the death.
To regain honour and self-respect,
I'll be a woman and fill your heart with tenderness
And I'll be a man to gain respect.

SEGISMUNDO. God if it's true I'm dreaming
Then stop me remembering
For it's not possible for so many things
All to fit into the one dream!
God help me! Is there anyone
Who could solve all those dilemmas
Or else turn his back on all of them!
All the things she said . . . !
If I was really dreaming I was king
Then how come that woman saw me
And can tell me about it in such detail?
So it has to have been true.
It can't have been a dream.
But if it was true, then it just makes

Everything far more confusing.
Because how come I think
My life's a dream? I mean,
Are wonderful experiences so like dreams
That what's real can be utterly dreamlike
And what's unreal can be taken to be true?
Which means, which means it must be obvious
That this dream is what life is
And that this life is really just a dream.
So if that's true, and all this greatness
All this majesty, all this power,
If it's all going to disappear as if it never was
The thing to do is make the most of what we've got.
I've got Rosaura in my power
And I love her incredible beauty
So let's make the most of it.
It's true she trusts me, she expects me to help her
But I want her. And love and desire
Break all rules of confidence and trust.
If everything's just a dream,
Then let's dream, my soul,
Let's dream of happiness
Because we know it will soon be grief.
But I've just gone and made myself
Change my mind. There has to be
A kind of happiness that lasts for ever.
And who'd want to destroy that
Just for a moment's pleasure?
Every past happiness is just a dream.
Is there anyone here who hasn't
Thought back to some happy time
And thought: 'It all feels like

It was just a dream?' There's a thought
That kills all illusion, there's a thought
Makes every pleasure seem like a candle flame
Easily blown out by the first breath of wind.
I have to look for more than that
I have to look for something that lasts for ever
Some living, ever-burning flame
Where happiness never ends
And great things are not forgotten.
And anyway, when I look at Rosaura . . .
I'm more in love with her than ever,
But I don't know . . . Her story's placed
Some kind of poison in my soul.
It's the thought her body's already been enjoyed
By someone else. What a vile thing
It must be in this world to love
Someone another has forgotten, to love
Someone another still enjoys! Besides,
Rosaura has been dishonoured.
A good prince should not dishonour her more
A good prince should give her honour back.
For God's sake, that's what I should try to regain
That's more important than gaining power!
But I'll have to turn my back on this opportunity
Because it's just so very attractive . . .

Sound to arms! We'll fight the battle today!
To arms! To arms!

ROSAURA.   My lord
Why do you turn your back on me?
Don't all my troubles even earn
A single word? How can you bear

To turn your back on me?
Not to look at me or hear me?
Won't you even turn a moment
Won't you even give me a single glance?

SEGISMUNDO. Rosaura, I want to show you pity
So for now I must be cruel.
I want to answer with my actions
I dare not answer with my voice.
I cannot look at you because
In such uncertain, dangerous times
Anyone who wants to think about your honour
Cannot afford to gaze upon your beauty.

Exit SEGISMUNDO *and the* SOLDIERS.

ROSAURA. O for god's sake! What's that supposed to
    be about!
After all I've gone through
And I've still got to cope
With such incomprehensible replies?

Enter CLARIN.

CLARIN. My lady, can I see you?

ROSAURA. Oh Clarín! Where have you been?

CLARIN. Locked up in a tower. Playing cards with death.
She almost played me a nasty trick
And I was very nearly disappeared.

ROSAURA. Why?

CLARIN. Because I know the secret of who you are
And your father is. And that in fact Clotaldo . . .

Drums beat within.

But what is that appalling noise?

ROSAURA. What can it be?

CLARIN. Oh it's just an armed regiment coming out
    Of the besieged palace to try to beat
    The fearsome army of fierce Segismundo.

ROSAURA. Then what am I doing standing here like
      a coward?
    Why aren't I out there fighting beside him
    Scandalising the entire world
    When there's so much violence and cruelty
    Tearing the world apart without order and law?

    Exit.

WITHIN SOME VOICES. Long live our King!

WITHIN SOME OTHER VOICES. Long live our freedom!

CLARIN. Long live our freedom! And long live the king!
    Let them both live very happily together
    Because nothing's going to bother me at all
    Just as long as I'm on the winning side at the end.
    But just for now I think I'll make myself scarce.
    I don't fancy playing a soldier at all.
    I think I'll play Nero instead.
    I'll just buy a violin second hand
    And play fiddle while Poland burns.
    And I really won't care what happens
    Just as long as it all leaves me alone.
    There's a little snug crevice here
    In among these rocks.
    To hell with death.
    She'll never find me here.

He hides. We hear the sound of clashing weapons, and then enter the
KING, CLOTALDO *and* ASTOLFO, *all running away.*

BASILIO. Was there ever a more unfortunate king?
  Was there ever a more mistreated father?

CLOTALDO. Your defeated army flees without order
    or discipline.

ASTOLFO. The battlefield belongs to the rebellious traitors.

BASILIO. In battles like these, Astolfo,
  The loyal subjects are those who win
  The rebellious traitors are those who lose.

A shot within. CLARIN *falls, wounded, from where he is.*

BASILIO. Who is it?

ASTOLFO. Who is this wretched soldier
  Falling at our feet
  Wounded and covered in blood?

CLARIN. I'm someone who wanted to run from death
  But all I did was find it.
  That's how it is; you run
  From the thing you're afraid of
  And you run right into it.
  You try to avoid it, but
  Instead you make it happen.
  You're trying to escape death
  On the battlefield by running
  Deep into the deserted mountains
  But turn back. Turn back!
  You're safer among gunshots
  In less danger from sword thrusts

Than in the remotest valley.
There is nowhere safe, nowhere
To escape the reach of death.
Remember you're going to die
If God says your hour has come.

He falls within.

BASILIO. Remember that you're going to die
If God says your hour has come.
O God how well this speaking corpse
How well this wounded bleeding mouth
Persuades us of our ignorance and error.
His trail of blood is like a tongue
Teaching us that when we try to resist a higher power
Everything we do is wasted effort.
I tried to prevent my country suffering
Rebellion bloodshed and civil war
And all I've done is to create the very suffering
I worked so hard to try to prevent.

CLOTALDO. My lord, it's true that death knows every
     path
But a good Christian does not despair
And say there's no escaping evil destiny.
It isn't true; the wise and prudent man
Can control his destiny, can control his fate.
At the moment you are not at all protected
From danger and calamity; so you must take steps
And find a place where you can be safe.

ASTOLFO. Clotaldo, my lord, speaks to you
As a prudent man of advancing age.
I speak to you as a brave young man

Who has kept a fast horse hidden in the mountain.
It's a swift abortion of the dawn:
Take it and ride away on it;
For I will guard your back.

BASILIO. If God has decreed I die
    Or if death lies in wait for me
    I want to meet it here.
    And meet death face to face.

Weapons clash; enter SEGISMUNDO *and the whole*
COMPANY.

SEGISMUNDO. The king is hiding in the mountains
    In the thick branches of the forest.
    Follow him. Search the forest
    Tree by tree and leaf by leaf.

CLOTALDO. Your majesty, run!

BASILIO. Why?

ASTOLFO. What do you intend to do?

BASILIO. Get back Astolfo!

CLOTALDO. What do you intend?

BASILIO. To do the thing that I must do.
    If it's me you're looking for
    Then here I am. I kneel before you.
    I lie on the ground and I'm helpless at your feet.
    Here I am. Trample me in the mud.
    Use me as your slave.
    And after so many attempts to evade it
    Let the will of fate be done
    Let the decree of heaven be fulfilled.

SEGISMUNDO. Famous court of Poland
      Witness of so many amazing events
      Listen to me: I speak to you as your Prince.
      God writes our stories with his finger in the sky
      And he writes with letters of silver and gold
      On the beautiful azure of heaven's mysteries.
      God never lies; the man who lies,
      The man who deceives,
      Is the man who deciphers these mysteries
      And then makes wrong use of them.
      Look at my father, who feared my rage
      And then did everything to provoke it.
      He made me wild beast, a brute, when
      Everything in my heritage
      Predisposed me to be gentle and courteous.
      But because he treated me like an animal
      I became a savage beast.
      What kind of wisdom was that!
      If someone said to you:
      'Be careful of that animal. Its lucky it's sleeping
      Because it's savage and cruel
      And would certainly kill you
      If you wake it.' Would it be wise
      To take a sharpened stick and poke it?
      If someone said to you:
      'Be careful of that sword you're wearing
      Or its sharp blade will kill you'
      Would it be wise to unsheathe it
      And hold its naked point against your chest?
      And what if someone said:
      'Be careful of the ocean deeps:
      Or its depths will be your gravestone'

Would it be wise to take a boat
And set out from harbour in the middle of a storm?
My rage was that sleeping beast
My fury that sheathed sword
My cruelty that stormy sea.
If life threatens you with evil
It cannot be overcome
By acting with injustice and cruelty
For that only increases its malice.
It can only be defeated
By courage intelligence and strength,
Daring to meet evil face to face.
All of you: observe the downfall of this king
Witness this extraordinary spectacle
Let it fill you with fear and amazement.
My father did everything he could
To escape an evil that threatened him
And failed. So how can I
Not so old as he, not so brave and not so wise
How can I do any better?
Father please get up, don't lie there on the ground.
Give me your hand, and now
Heaven and the world have shown you your mistakes
I bow my head, I kneel at your feet
And I place myself at your mercy.

BASILIO. My son, in your nobility you are reborn.
You are prince; the laurel and the palm of victory
Are yours. You overcame. Your achievements
Give you victory.

ALL.   Long live Segismundo!

SEGISMUNDO. There are more victories I need to win
    And they all require great courage.
    I'll start with the hardest: to overcome myself.
    I have decided to restore Rosaura's honour:
    So Astolfo you must marry her at once.

ASTOLFO. Although it's true I owe her obligations
    I have to say her father is unknown.
    Clearly it would be baseness and infamy
    For me to marry such a woman.

CLOTALDO. Stop. that's enough, don't go on.
    For Rosaura is as noble as you are,
    And my sword will defend her in a duel.
    She's my daughter. That's all that need be said.

ASTOLFO. What?

CLOTALDO.   Until she was married and honourable
    I didn't want to reveal who she was.
    The story of this is very long
    But there you are. She is my daughter.

ASTOLFO. Well, if that's the case I'll keep my promise.

ROSAURA. In one day, I've found a double happiness.

SEGISMUNDO. And so I need to marry Estrella
    To a Prince of equal rank and worth.
    I'll marry you myself. Give me your hand.

ESTRELLA. I seem to have got myself a better husband.

SEGISMUNDO. And Clotaldo, as a reward for loyalty,
    Will be my Chief Minister.

SOLDIER 1. So if you're rewarding all these people

Who fought against you and did you harm
What will you give me, who started this rebellion
Set you free from the tower and made you king?

SEGISMUNDO. The tower. And there you'll stay
Chained up until you die.
For once the moment of betrayal's past
It's important to get rid of the traitor.

ASTOLFO. How very wise!

BASILIO.   What statesmanship!

CLOTALDO. How much you've changed!

ROSAURA. How clever you've become!

SEGISMUNDO. Why are you all so amazed? I still live
    in dread
I'm going to wake up and find myself in prison again.
My teacher was a dream
A dream that destroys illusions
And tells me life's just a sweet lie
And when we wake up from it
We find it's nothing. Empty air.
It's how it is for an actor,
One minute he's a king
And the next he's at your mercy.
When the play comes to its end
He humbly begs your pardon
And asks you to forgive mistakes.

End.